A Beginner's Guide to Doing Your Education Research Project

Education at SAGE

SAGE is a leading international publisher of journals, books, and electronic media for academic, educational, and professional markets.

Our education publishing includes:

- accessible and comprehensive texts for aspiring education professionals and practitioners looking to further their careers through continuing professional development

- inspirational advice and guidance for the classroom

- authoritative state of the art reference from the leading authors in the field

Find out more at: **www.sagepub.co.uk/education**

A Beginner's Guide to Doing Your Education Research Project

Mike Lambert

SSAGE

Los Angeles | London | New Delhi
Singapore | Washington DC

Los Angeles | London | New Delhi
Singapore | Washington DC

SAGE Publications Ltd
1 Oliver's Yard
55 City Road
London EC1Y 1SP

SAGE Publications Inc.
2455 Teller Road
Thousand Oaks, California 91320

SAGE Publications India Pvt Ltd
B 1/I 1 Mohan Cooperative Industrial Area
Mathura Road
New Delhi 110 044

SAGE Publications Asia-Pacific Pte Ltd
3 Church Street
#10-04 Samsung Hub
Singapore 049483

Editor: Jude Bowen
Editorial assistant: Miriam Davey
Project manager: Jeanette Graham
Assistant production editor: Thea Watson
Copyeditor: Sharon Cawood
Proofreader: Salia Nessa
Marketing manager: Lorna Patkai
Cover design: Wendy Scott
Typeset by: C&M Digitals (P) Ltd, Chennai, India
Printed by: CPI Group (UK) Ltd, Croydon, CR0 4YY

MIX
Paper from
responsible sources
FSC
www.fsc.org   FSC® C013604

First published 2012

Library of Congress Control Number: 2012933234

British Library Cataloguing in Publication data

A catalogue record for this book is available from the British Library

ISBN 978-0-85702-980-5
ISBN 978-0-85702-981-2 (pbk)

Contents

List of figures

List of photocopiables

These can all be found in Appendix I.

About the author

Dr Mike Lambert is Principal Lecturer in Education at the University of Wolverhampton, England. He developed and teaches the university's Research Methods module for initial teacher training, and has supervised the projects of many students at undergraduate and postgraduate levels. Previously, he taught in a variety of schools, with particular interest in the education of students with special educational needs and disabilities, and worked internationally for voluntary organizations in this field. Mike's doctorate focused on pedagogy for gifted students. He contributes regularly to professional and academic publications on education and research.

Acknowledgements

I am grateful to reviewers and colleagues who commented on drafts, and also to the University of Wolverhampton for support which enabled me to write this book. Thank you in particular to the many students whose ideas and experiences have inspired its contents and case studies. All names have been changed, of course, but some may recognize situations described in the text.

Thank you, too, to Jude Bowen and Miriam Davey at Sage for their ever-ready assistance and advice. Finally, thank you to my wife, Tunde, whose guidance and constant support contributed so much to this book's completion.

Note to students (and tutors)

This book is based on my experiences supervising undergraduate and postgraduate projects, teaching research methods and carrying out research of my own. It presents the process of doing a research project (as a book has to do) in a linear format – start at the beginning and work through to the end. However, in reality research is more complex than this – you twist and turn, move back and forth, and rarely find your work progressing in a straightforward way.

I would encourage you, therefore, to get to know this book as a whole while working through each of its chapters in turn. For instance, some familiarity with validity and reliability (Chapter 9) and data analysis (Chapter 11) will help you to make decisions about methodology (Chapter 7), and an awareness of how the final written project is presented (Chapter 12) will help the drafting of text at earlier stages. Consideration of ethics, as I have sought to convey, applies at all stages, of course.

The guidance presented is not the only advice which you will be taking into account. As a researcher, you may wish to pursue paths of your own; tutors will guide you towards other routes too, especially where they disagree (as they sometimes will) with recommendations provided here. Throughout the book, therefore, you are encouraged to read widely and to consult with your project or supervising tutor on the progress of your work. When advice differs, I would encourage you to make decisions in relation to your own circumstances, and more formally to your course and tutorial guidance, as this is the basis on which your project will be assessed.

I welcome feedback from all readers on ways in which this book might be strengthened further to help those undertaking a research project in education for the first time.

Mike Lambert
University of Wolverhampton, UK
m.lambert@wlv.ac.uk

Introduction

What will you learn from this chapter?

In this introduction, we consider the importance of educational research, then look at the purpose of this book and for whom it is written. I explain the book's structure and its contents and how it relates to your taught course of study. Overall, this chapter prepares you for thinking in detail about your research project in education.

Research: important or just interesting?

Research is important – it is all around us, it influences (even changes) our lives, the lives of children who follow us, and the lives of their children too. Or is it? Research into smoking, for instance, has altered our understanding of healthy behaviour, but many people still smoke anyway. Research into road accidents has changed car design and the laws we follow, but drivers continue to drive in different ways. So is research important, or is it just interesting?

What about research into education? The picture here too is mixed. Many publications are devoted to educational research and governments often refer to its findings to justify their actions. Investigations also create plenty of heated discussion: What is the best way to teach? How do children and adults best learn? Some, however (including you, perhaps), might claim that education does not need all that research, and that most professionals do not pay much attention to it anyway. Common sense and a feel for good educational practice may ultimately be more important than knowing anything about research.

Research and you

You may not, therefore, be fully convinced by the idea of doing a research project. Let me therefore persuade you of its value, and in doing so, show also the merit of reading this book:

1 **Work in education is a complicated business**: In education you do a hundred different things every day. You work with colleagues, parents

and carers, and others. You help children and young people to make progress, manage their behaviour, encourage motivation and support them through difficult times.

2 **Learning is even more complicated**: The children and students you work with are different from each other and from you. They have a range of backgrounds, values and opinions. Yet, in most cases, they learn together and need to learn the same kinds of things.

3 **Educators are ultimately in charge**: In the classroom, children and students may engage in collaborative learning, paired talk, shared investigation or other activities where they take on responsibility for their own learning. In the end, however, adult educators are always responsible for what goes on.

With any intricate matter, we need time and effort to understand it well (think, for instance, of improving a complex machine, or making sense of the weather). That is the case I make for those in education engaging in research. Put quite simply, helping others to learn and develop is a complicated affair. Common sense gets me a long way, but it will not tell me everything. To be a knowledgeable and effective educator, I have to dig deeper, find out more, and learn from the experiences of others who have dug deeper too. Doing this will make me more informed, more knowledgeable about learning, more analytical and more critical of my own practice and the practice of others, more ready, able and willing to improve. It will give the students for whom I am responsible better opportunity to learn successfully.

 Key Points

> Doing research helps us to understand better the complicated business of education. Investigation helps us to appraise our own practice and the practice of others, and to strengthen the learning of those for whom we have responsibility.

Education: a research-based profession?

At an important lecture in 1996, Professor David Hargreaves considered the place of research in education: 'Teaching is not at present a research-based profession. I have no doubt that if it were, teaching would be more effective and more satisfying' (Hargreaves, 2007: 3). He compared practitioner research in the field of medicine with the need for 'evidence-informed practice' in schools and elsewhere: 'In education we too need evidence about what works with whom under what conditions and with what effects' (2007: 13).

Not everyone agreed at the time, and debate on the issue has continued since then. The collection by Hammersley (2007) (in which the Hargreaves lecture is reprinted) shows the range of arguments about the role of educators in researching their own practice and that of others. However, this idea has taken root and doing research is now generally seen as an important part of development for all education professionals and for the institutions where they work.

Why this book?

Research itself is another intricate puzzle – at least it often looks that way. There are many decisions to make: What to investigate? How to investigate it? Who to involve? How to find answers? In doing an education research project, you are using one complicated process (doing research) to investigate another (education). No wonder that it can be a daunting prospect for beginner researchers – and often for those with more experience also.

The project you are undertaking is likely to be based on the idea of a practical investigation, using some of the common features and approaches of formal research. This might include tasks such as reviewing relevant literature, choosing and using appropriate research methods, and writing up your results in a formal report. You may also need to get 'ethical approval' to carry out your investigation, work independently, attend tutorials with a supervising tutor and ensure that the work you produce is your own, not 'plagiarized' from the work of others. This book helps you step by step through all these aspects and more.

This may be the first time that you have been required to tackle a research project like this. The task may seem very different to other pieces of written work you have already completed on your course of study. It may look, therefore, like a considerable challenge. This book will help you to meet this challenge, produce a worthwhile project, and be ready (and perhaps keen) to move on to more sophisticated research as a continuing postgraduate student or reflective, investigative professional.

How this book relates to your course

Whatever its value, this book is not a total substitute for all the other ways you learn about how to tackle your project. If you are on an undergraduate or postgraduate course, you will also be learning from:

- attendance, participation and note-taking at lectures or taught sessions
- course material about how to do your project

- tutorial sessions and discussions with a supervising 'project tutor' probably assigned to you
- your own independent study and investigation, including reading other books about doing research.

There may be instances where the advice given in this book is not the same as that given by your tutors, your course material or indeed your own views. This is not unusual – there are many different ways of tackling research.

 Key Points

> If the advice given in this book is not the same as that given by your tutor or your course material, it is usually best to follow your course guidance, as that is how your written project will be assessed. Alternatively, you should discuss and clarify discrepancies with your project tutor at a tutorial.

Structure and contents

This book is structured to reflect the process by which you will plan, carry out and write up your research. When you read it, you will most probably wish to start at the beginning and work your way through from one chapter to the next. However, research is not such a linear process, and I would encourage you also to look at chapters out of order when it helps. Jump ahead if a theme is relevant or interesting for you, or is being covered in your course at the time. Also look back to remind yourself of what you have already seen and to work out how different aspects of a project relate to each other.

This then is how the book is laid out:

Introduction

This is what you are reading now. I am setting out the purpose and structure of this book and how it relates to your project and to your taught course of study.

Chapter 1: Research, 'paradigms' and ethics

Chapter 1 explains how research creates deeper understanding and helps education professionals to work successfully with children and young people. It illustrates the variety of research activity which can be undertaken and what might be suitable for your own project. We also consider the important role of 'ethics', whereby you, the researcher, ensure at every stage that the investigation is not causing disadvantage or harm to those involved.

Chapter 2: The process of doing research

This important chapter provides an overview of the research process, from the drawing up of a rough idea for investigation, through to completing and submitting the final written research dissertation. It helps you to get a picture of your task as a whole.

Chapter 3: Learning from other research

Chapter 3 sets you an optional task. This involves finding and examining a piece of research which has already been published, identifying different aspects of this research and relating its findings to educational practice. Doing this task will help you understand more about the processes of investigation and will prepare you for undertaking your own project.

Chapter 4: Choosing your topic

Now starts the step-by-step process by which you will tackle your project. Chapter 4 considers the first of these steps: choosing a suitable educational topic for investigation and justifying this choice. It explains how you can limit the focus of this topic so you can scrutinize an issue in depth and, in so doing, produce an informative and valuable study.

Chapter 5: Research questions

The next chapter explains what 'research questions' are and how they are important for the success of your whole project. It shows how you can design them, highlighting features of good questions and what should be avoided.

Chapter 6: Literature review

'Literature' means the books, articles and other published material which have already been written about your topic. You will need to show an understanding of this literature in your project. The chapter explains how you can find relevant material, examine it, and present your analysis in a structured, organized and informative way.

Chapter 7: Choosing your methods

This chapter examines the principal methods you can use to investigate your topic, such as questionnaires, interviews and observations, and gives guidance on deciding which to choose.

Chapter 8: Designing your research instruments

Research instruments are the tools and resources you use when carrying out your investigation. Designing them well is crucial to getting useful data which answer your research questions. This chapter considers various ways in which you can design these for the methods you have chosen.

Chapter 9: Validity, reliability and ethical approval

This chapter helps you to understand some further concepts which you must consider, including the vital step of getting formal ethical approval to start your investigation.

Chapter 10: Carrying out your investigation

This chapter provides advice on how you can carry out your practical investigation in an effective and professional way.

Chapter 11: Analysing data and producing your findings

Chapter 11 looks at how you can examine your data and produce clear, interesting and useful findings which answer your research questions – the ultimate reason for doing research.

Chapter 12: Writing up your project

Chapter 12 shows how you can put together each section of your final written text, paying close attention to content, structure, style, presentation, referencing and accurate use of English.

Conclusion

The conclusion to this book encourages you to consider how you can share with others the deeper understanding you have gained from your investigation.

Appendices

The appendices provide a series of Project Sheets for developing your project, answers for activities, and a glossary of key research terms used in this book.

Features

This book also has a range of pedagogical features, which will strengthen your interaction with the text and provide different routes to greater understanding. These include:

What will I learn from this chapter?

This summarizes what you will gain from the chapter in relation to the development of your project.

 ### Project Sheets

Photocopiable Project Sheets are provided for all stages of your work in Appendix I. They help you to build up your research and write draft text as you go along which will feed into your final written project. They are also available online at Sage Methodspace: www.methodspace.com/group/mikelambert.

 ### Activities

These activities are based on simple situations, or on aspects of the research process itself. Some you can do in just one or two minutes, while others are more substantial. They can usually be done individually or by a small group of readers working together. Model answers are provided in Appendix II.

Further reading

When doing your project, you should consult a range of reading about doing research. This will enable you to learn from different opinions and approaches. Take note, therefore, of the literature I refer to in the text itself, then make use of the further reading I recommend at the end of each chapter.

Glossary

There are definitions of many key research terms in the text. These are collected together in a glossary in Appendix III.

Referencing

Referencing is an important aspect of any research investigation. I use references in all chapters, so you can see how to do this in your own work, and also to guide you towards useful material on how to do research. The referencing system used in this book is based on the 'Harvard' system, which means that the family name of the author and year of publication are provided in the text, then full details are provided in a reference list at the end.

I have already started to reference published material in this way. For instance, in the short section about education as a research-based profession, I referenced (or 'cited') two pieces of work: Hargreaves (2007) and Hammersley (2007). I did this because the ideas I was writing about were not my own – I was taking them from work written by others. I therefore needed to show this. Referencing ideas taken from other sources is essential good practice in academic writing.

You will see also that I have included both of these publications in a reference list at the end of this book. Because the list is in alphabetical order, you can easily find the full details of these and of other material cited in this book. When you put together your research project, you will need to reference in a similar way (although you may be required to use a different referencing system). We deal with this in full in Chapter 12. There is computer software available which helps to organize and present citations correctly, for example EndNote or RefWorks. However, it is unlikely that as a beginner researcher you will find these worthwhile. I recommend instead that you keep careful, accurate manual notes from the start to ensure clarity and accuracy in your referencing.

Time to start

You are ready now to think in more detail about research and about your own project. We begin in the next chapter with a closer look at the nature of research and at the vital concept of ethics. By doing a research project, you are joining a rich community of investigation and discovery, which aims to strengthen understanding, improve society and – in your case – enhance the learning and lives of children, students and other learners. It is time to start.

SECTION ONE

Learning about Research

1 Research, 'paradigms' and ethics

What will you learn from this chapter?

This first chapter examines what research is and describes some different types. It guides you towards choosing an appropriate kind of research for your own project. We also consider 'paradigms' – the different kinds of thinking which underlie research activity – and 'ethics', a very important theme which we will regularly discuss in this book. Finally, I encourage you to feel positive about the challenge of doing your investigation, and highlight what you will gain from it.

What is research?

Research is all around us – we do it in our daily lives all the time:

- Before we go shopping, we look in cupboards to find out what we need to buy.
- When we want to give someone a present, we ask friends or family what that person might like to receive.
- When we want to study on a course, we examine possibilities on the Internet before deciding which one to apply for.

We rely on more formal research for organizing and improving human activity:

- We rely on medical research to make sure that medicines are safe and effective.

- We rely on consumer research so that what we want to buy is available in the shops.
- We rely on social research for planning the growth of our institutions and services.

With this range of types of research, the notion of research itself is not easy to pin down. Sharp (2009: 3) defined it simply as 'finding things out' and Mukherji and Albon (2010: 10) as 'seeking information to answer the questions that we pose'. Here is my definition:

 Key Points

Research is purposeful investigation, aimed at finding out things we did not know before.

Rather than one single definition, however, it is more informative to draw up a series of statements which describe research at various levels:

1 At its simplest:
   - research is a planned investigation, carried out in an organized and systematic way
   - it produces information (called 'data') which, when analysed, tells us things we did not know or were unsure about before
   - when applied to practice, this new understanding may influence what we do.

2 Thinking further, research involves:
   - asking questions at the start of the investigation
   - collecting data, then using these data to answer the questions.

3 At a third level, research also involves:
   - connecting the investigation to what is already known about its topic
   - looking carefully and critically at how we collect information, to see if we can trust what it tells us
   - presenting what we find out in clear, precise and persuasive ways, so that others can learn more or gain better understanding of the topic we have investigated.

We can continue constructing levels to describe what research is about. The more we have, the closer we are to the kind of academic research which you should be aiming for in your project. Blaxter et al. (2001: 5) summarized it well more than a decade ago: '[All types of research] are, or aim to be, planned, cautious, systematic, and reliable ways of finding out or deepening understanding'.

Research is also often seen as a formal aspect of educators' 'reflective practice'. Being 'reflective' means thinking hard about what you do, assessing its value and working out how things might be done better. It is helped by 'competence in methods of evidence-based classroom enquiry' (Pollard, 2008: 14), that is, an understanding of how to do research. This allows practitioners to adopt more structured approaches to appraisal of practice, to take into account what other investigations have found out, and to think more rigorously, relying more on evidence and less on impression and anecdote.

 Activity 1.1   Understanding 'research'

Bring up a thesaurus on your computer:

* In Microsoft Word, press Shift + F7
* With Apple, press ctrl + alt + cmd + R
* Or use http://thesaurus.com

Type the word 'research' in the Search box, and press Enter. See what other words come up. Click on these words to find further associated terms. What do all these words tell you about the meaning and features of 'research'?

Categorizing research

We can categorize research in many different ways. For instance, it is carried out at different levels: undergraduate, practitioner, Masters, doctoral and post-doctoral. It may be funded by an external body, including government, or not have any allocated financial support at all. It can also relate to a wide range of themes, including (of course) education.

Educational research investigates learning, curriculum and educational practice. It can be carried out by practitioners or by 'outsiders' (and even by children and school students themselves). It may achieve many things – your project may achieve these too. For example, it can:

* strengthen understanding of how centres, schools or colleges function and how they might function better
* deepen understanding of educational practice, in the classroom and elsewhere

- explore the feelings ('perspectives') of those in education about curriculum, styles of teaching and about learning itself.

It also comes in different forms. Here are some common approaches, together with examples of each:

Theoretical research

Theoretical research scrutinizes concepts and ideas (such as equality and justice), rather than their practical application.

Example: *Starting his discussion with: 'Teachers often shut their students up', Callan (2011) examined the tensions between the silencing of students' derogatory comments and the ideals of free speech.*

Action or practitioner research

Action research investigates everyday actions, in work or in our social lives, with a view to improving systems and practice. It is often carried out by practitioners, such as teachers. Participants themselves may also have direct input into design and monitoring of the investigation (sometimes known as 'participatory' research).

Example: *Rule and Modipa (2011) explored the educational experiences of adults with disabilities in South Africa. The study's participatory, action-research approach involved people with disabilities designing and conducting the investigation. The study was also an example of 'emancipatory research' which challenges social oppression of marginalized groups.*

Evaluative

Evaluative research assesses the usefulness or effectiveness of an organization or activity, possibly to indicate whether this should be continued.

Example: *Blenkinsop et al. (2007) evaluated the School Fruit and Vegetable Scheme, which provided fruit to young children in English schools every morning. They found that children's fruit consumption increased, but saw no wider or sustained impact on their diet.*

Experimental

This involves a structured experiment. Situations are carefully organized, so that different scenarios can be investigated. For instance, two student groups (one 'experimental', the other 'control') are taught the same thing in different ways. The researcher then tries to determine which approach is more beneficial. To adopt this approach, it must be possible to measure clearly the issue in question.

Example: *Finnish research by Iivonen, Sääkslahti and Nissinen (2011) used two groups of young children to study the effects of an eight-month, pre-school, physical-education curriculum.*

'Cause and effect' research

Experimental research is usually associated with what I call 'cause and effect' research – trying to find out if and how one thing causes or affects another. For instance, does a particular teaching approach, initiative or resource improve students' learning and achievement?

Example: *Blatchford et al. (2011) studied over 8000 students to examine the effects of work by education support staff. Uncomfortably for educators, it found that the students getting most support tended to make less academic progress than similar students with less support.*

Case study

Case-study research involves in-depth investigation of an individual, group, event or system, usually within its real-life context and sometimes over a period of time (called a 'longitudinal' study).

Example: *Forrester (2010) used a longitudinal case-study approach to document the musical development of one child between the ages of 1 and 4 years.*

Systematic review

Systematic reviews critically appraise a range of research evidence or literature (or both) on a particular topic. From the analysis, it identifies key messages and continuing gaps in understanding.

Example: *Sebba et al. (2008) searched electronic databases and journals to find and review 26 published research studies relating to the topic of self and peer assessment in secondary schools.*

Exploratory

Exploratory research seeks to understand situations more clearly and deeply than before, often from varied perspectives.

Example: *Rassool (2004) explored ways in which children from minority ethnic groups viewed themselves culturally and educationally within British society.*

Comparative

Comparative research investigates two or more different situations, for instance practice in different countries or institutions, and makes comparisons in order to understand both situations better.

Example: *Jerman and Pretnar (2006) compared the musical abilities of 11-year-old children on the Caribbean island of Martinique and in Slovenia. This comparison identified common elements and some differences which seemed to explain much better results on Martinique.*

Grounded theory

This approach is often used to create or produce an overall theory from wide-ranging investigation, often culminating in an intricate flow chart or diagram. The approach was first formulated by Glaser and Strauss (1967).

Example: *Thornberg's (2008) grounded-theory research in Sweden developed a categorized system of school rules and sought to explain the logic behind them.*

Ethnography

Ethnographic research studies cultures or groups in naturalistic contexts, 'understanding things from the point of view of those involved' (Denscombe, 2010: 80–81). Ethnographic researchers often immerse themselves in the lives of those they are researching.

Example: *Tang and Maxwell (2007) used observation, interviews, daily conversations and questionnaires to investigate cultural features of the Chinese kindergarten curriculum, finding that 'children are taught to learn together rather than explore individually' and that children's 'spontaneous learning interests are welcomed but seldom developed in depth'.*

 Activity 1.2   Types of research

Find a research journal in your library or research reports on the Internet (see the further reading at the end of this chapter for a possible source). Scan the articles and identify what kind of research has been carried out.

Choosing your type of research

The categorization above is not definitive – research can be described in different ways. Compare my list, for instance, with that provided by Walliman (2011: 8–21), or in other books about research. Different approaches may also be combined. For instance, cause-and-effect and experimental research are closely connected; action research can be ethnographic in nature; exploratory research may be associated with a grounded-theory approach and can be comparative when two or more situations are investigated. For your project, you could theoretically adopt any of the approaches described above, or indeed others not listed here. However, you should think carefully about what is manageable and possible, given the scale of your study and your level of research expertise. Here is my advice on some of the categories outlined above:

Theoretical: Researching ideas is not straightforward – it involves scrutinising ways of thinking and writing analytically about them. It is not usually an appropriate option for beginner researchers.

Action or practitioner research: Many reading this book will be close to the action of the classroom in one way or another. It is likely that you wish to use your research to strengthen understanding of educational practice, and therefore your approach may well be of this kind.

Evaluative: Evaluative research usually involves judging the quality of educational practice and being ready to make objective, critical comment. This may be difficult or inappropriate to do, especially if you are a student on work placement or teaching practice.

Experimental: To carry out an experiment you will need to set up two or more research environments, for instance two similar groups of children taught in different ways. You will need to control other factors (these are called 'variables') – for example, the material being taught and physical environment – so that the teaching approach you are investigating is as far as possible the only difference between the groups. This is usually beyond the scope of undergraduate researchers, although it may be feasible for a practising teacher who is able to organize groups in this way. Note that because of ethical concerns (which we start to examine below) one group should not be knowingly disadvantaged by your investigation.

Cause and effect: This is a tempting approach to take – most educators want to find out the impact of different kinds of educational work. However, this too is difficult. There are simply too many alternative explanations for any 'effect' that may be indicated by the investigation. It may, however, be possible to identify 'indications' or 'perceptions' of impact, rather than seeking confirmation or proof (we examine this possible approach when we discuss choosing your topic in Chapter 4).

Case study: The term 'case study' is used rather loosely to describe defined, small-scale research. More strictly, however, it is a specific research strategy, with its own underlying principles. If you think you will be doing a case study, consult relevant literature on this, for instance Yin (2009) and Simons (2009).

Systematic review: Most projects require students to undertake active collection of data 'in the field': observing, interviewing, using questionnaires, and so on. A systematic review will not meet these requirements. If a review is possible, this should be stated in your course documentation. If in doubt, discuss with your project tutor.

Exploratory: Combining action research with an exploratory approach may be the most appropriate kind of project for the beginner researcher. You explore an aspect of educational practice to deepen your own understanding and inform that of others. Many examples in this book are of this kind.

Comparative: Take care if you decide on this kind of research. It doubles your work because everything you do in one situation you need to repeat in the other. Also be clear in your own mind why you are making the comparison. If you wish to determine which approach or situation is 'better' or 'more effective', then you are coming close to experimental research, described above, and the difficulties associated with it. Instead, you could use your comparison to strengthen an exploratory approach and achieve a fuller picture of the issue as a whole.

 Key Points

In summary:

1 Check your course documentation to see if it stipulates what kind of research is required for your project.
2 If possible, discuss the nature of your research with your project tutor early in your course.
3 Make sure also that the type of investigation you choose will be manageable and appropriate for beginner research.

'Paradigms'

If you have already done some reading about research, you may have discovered that different kinds of investigation tend to reflect different research 'paradigms'. Perhaps you were rather mystified by what this meant. Sharp (2009: 5) agreed: 'It's all a bit tricky to the initiated never mind the uninitiated'.

The first thing about paradigms is not to lose sleep about them. As a beginner researcher, you can put together a coherent and useful research project without understanding paradigms much at all. Nevertheless, some awareness is worthwhile – you can appreciate icebergs by seeing what is above the water, but they are more interesting when you also understand what lies beneath. In the same way, knowing something about paradigms will open up deeper understanding of your own research activity. Furthermore, the requirements for your course may require you to consider the issue of paradigms when putting together your own project. In this case, you must seek some understanding of this concept and its relation to your own investigation.

To start with, therefore, here are some definitions of the term in relation to research:

'Paradigms are models, perspectives or conceptual frameworks that help us to organize our thoughts, beliefs, views and practices into a logical whole' (Basit, 2010: 14).

'Paradigms reflect our underpinning assumptions about the nature of knowledge and the best ways of understanding the world around us' (Mukherji and Albon, 2010: 7).

My own definition is this:

 Key Points

> Paradigms are the conscious and subconscious beliefs which lie beneath the questions we ask and ways we carry out research, and which shape the kind of conclusions which emerge from our investigations.

Those definitions are not straightforward, so to understand them better, let us look at the two main paradigmatic 'schools' and some differences between them:

1. Positivist paradigm

Positivism is based on the idea that the world we are investigating has a stable and logical reality, and the purpose of investigation is to determine this and measure it. Human perception is not a reliable way of determining what this reality is – the researcher needs formal, systematic, 'truth-seeking' (Gray, 2009: 131) methods to find it out. A positivist paradigm is mostly associated with experimental and cause-and-effect research. It may also be called a 'normative' or 'scientific' paradigm.

2. Interpretivist paradigm

Interpretivism is different. Interpretivist (or 'naturalistic', or 'phenomenological') researchers do not believe that there is an external reality waiting to be discovered. Instead, they believe that what we accept as real arises from the different perceptions of different people, interacting with complex social and physical environments. Truth is socially 'constructed' – we decide (not always consciously) what it is – rather than existing independently of us. Research is therefore used to explore topics from various viewpoints (Gray, 2009: 31, calls it 'perspective- or opinion-seeking' research). An interpretivist researcher may build up several pictures of reality from those perspectives and put forward one or more possible interpretations or 'constructions' of an event or situation. In principle, another researcher could do similar research and produce a different construction, and if the research was well carried out, it could be as persuasive as the first.

As Gray (2009: 27) explains, therefore, the choice is 'whether the researcher believes there is some sort of external "truth" out there that needs discovering, or whether the task of research is to explore and unpick people's multiple perspectives in natural field settings'. There are other kinds of paradigms too, often adaptations or extensions of these two main types. Look out in your reading for 'pragmatism', 'feminism', 'post-structuralism' and others. There have been plenty of arguments about which is most appropriate – also look out for the term 'paradigm wars' to describe this vigorous debate. Fortunately, most researchers now take a more measured approach and may combine or integrate paradigms when undertaking research.

Your paradigm?

Paradigms, therefore, are about our view and understanding of the world. If you believe that reality is external to us and we can use formal research procedures to find out more about it, then you are likely to want to follow a positivist approach. You would collect 'firm' data – numbers and facts – for your investigation. If you believe that what is 'real' depends on how people perceive it, so that different 'realities' can co-exist, you are likely to want to follow an interpretivist approach. For your investigation, you would ask people about their experiences, beliefs and perceptions; you could also watch them working and interpret what you see.

In the end, you may find yourself drawing from both paradigms, combining collection of firm data with more flexible interpretation of experiences and perspectives. Whichever paradigm or paradigms inform your project, you may need to explain your standpoint when you write your project. So keep paradigms in mind and have a go at working out your own position if you can. This is especially the case when choosing your research methods in Chapter 7, as paradigms are a strong determinant of how you decide to do your investigation.

Key Points

In summary:

1 Knowing something about paradigms will strengthen your understanding of research.
2 Check with your course literature and project tutor about the extent to which you should consider your own paradigmatic position when planning and writing your project.
3 Do not worry too much about this concept, however. It will become clearer bit by bit. The more it does so, the more you will appreciate the thinking which lies beneath it.

Ethics

For beginner researchers, consideration of paradigms may be optional, but consideration of ethics is not. According to Oliver (2010: 15), research should 'avoid causing harm, distress, anxiety, pain or other negative feeling to participants'; for Alderson and Morrow (2011: 3), 'research ethics is concerned with respecting research participants throughout each project'. My own definition includes you as the researcher in this perspective as well:

 Key Points

Being 'ethical' means that your project does not bring harm or disadvantage to anyone who takes part, including yourself.

This sounds quite straightforward, but it is not. Often, what you want or need to do for your project is not desirable or appropriate for others. Here are some examples of the harm or disadvantage which your research could cause:

- **Disturbance:** Your investigation could interfere with the proper running of a class, or your wish to do interviews may disrupt a teacher's busy timetable.
- **Intrusion:** If you withdraw students for research work, they may miss an important lesson which will adversely affect their learning.
- **Secrecy:** If you keep secret from your participants what you are investigating, those participants may not realize the implications of what

they do or say. If they understood better, they may have preferred not to take part.

- **Embarrassment**: You may ask questions or make comments which cause embarrassment to your participants or to the organization where you are doing your research.
- **Lowering self-esteem**: Your research may highlight deficiencies or personal difficulties in your participants and lessen their status in front of colleagues, friends or you, the researcher.

Here too is one way in which your research may harm yourself:

- **Resentment**: In doing your research, you may ask too many personal questions, causing resentment amongst colleagues and adversely affecting your professional relationships.

As you may have realized already, you cannot avoid all such effects when doing research. Interviewing students, for instance, inevitably takes up time which they could be using for something else – however, this 'disruption' might turn out to be an interesting and beneficial break from routine. Some of the questions you ask could cause a degree of discomfort amongst your participants, but good research is often challenging, and most participants will recognize and cope perfectly well with this. Balance between investigation and the welfare of those taking part therefore needs to be found, with particular care taken if your research involves children, students and other potentially 'vulnerable' groups (see Chapter 9).

In the course of this book, therefore, we will discuss many aspects of ethics, such as confidentiality and anonymity, participants' 'informed consent' and your own professional behaviour as a researcher. We will find that 'ethical standards, high or low, weave into all parts of the research fabric and shape the methods and findings' (Alderson, 2004: 110). Oliver's (2010: 47) advice is vital: 'The principal matters, in an ethical sense, are that as researchers we take all reasonable measures to ensure the peace of mind, and fair treatment of the people we ask to help us with our research'.

Codes

There are various codes and guidelines which will help you to recognize ethical standards in your research. For instance:

- **BERA (British Educational Research Association)** BERA's ethical guidelines (www.bera.ac.uk) are the most important for UK researchers. They stress participants' right to privacy, to be informed about the research to which they are being asked to contribute and to withdraw from the investigation if they so wish. From researchers, they call for openness and attention to cultural and other differences.

- **Policies:** Relevant principles and procedures will be outlined in the policies of your research venue, the centre, school or college where you carry out your investigation. These include those for health and safety, student behaviour, Internet use and professional conduct. It is your responsibility as a researcher to seek out what is relevant for your work and to have regard to such policies when carrying out your investigation.

- **Course code and 'ethical approval':** It is also possible that your place of study has its own code or policies relating to ethical behaviour in research. Furthermore, you may need to apply for and get 'ethical approval' before commencing your investigation. We deal with this important procedure in Chapter 9.

 ## Activity 1.3   Understanding ethical principles

Below are some key ethical principles, informed by Pring (2004). Choose one or more of these to discuss with your colleagues: What do the principles mean? What implications does each have for research practice and your own investigation? What tensions underlie them – to what extent can a researcher work to all these principles at the same time?

1 Show respect for everyone who is helping you, as well as for those who decide that they do not wish to be involved.

2 Be ready to explain and discuss your research, and respond constructively to criticism about it.

3 Respect confidentiality of data and the anonymity of those taking part.

4 Take responsibility for what you do and for its consequences.

5 Take steps also to avoid situations which may cause harm to yourself.

6 Pursue truth in your investigation, but be aware of the implications of this for others and be 'tentative and modest' (Pring, 2004: 149) about what you claim to have discovered.

Let's move on

Doing research is not an easy option, but will bring you plenty of benefits. It will give you, as Thomas (2009: ix) points out, 'a questioning disposition, about evidence and the frailty of knowledge, about methods of research and their strengths and weaknesses'. It will help you combine a sense of independence with understanding of the views of others. It will mean you can grow as a reflective, constructively critical, motivated, even innovative member of the educational community as you progress in your work and career. Your project will be worth doing and worth doing well.

Are you persuaded? Even if you are, you are probably still uncertain about what you need to do to plan, develop and undertake a good research project. By working through this first chapter, however, you have made a useful start.

Later in this book, we will examine the steps of doing research one at a time. The next chapter and the optional task which follows in Chapter 3, however, look first at the process of research as a whole. What is your whole project like? What can you expect to achieve at the end of it? Let's move on.

Further reading 📖

Koshy, V. (2010) *Action Research for Improving Educational Practice: A Step-by-Step Guide*. 2nd ed. London: Sage.
A well-ordered and clearly presented guide to action research, a type of investigation which you may relate to your own project.

Mukherji, P. and Albon, D. (2010) *Research Methods in Early Childhood*. London: Sage.
Part 1 examines the nature of paradigms and the two main types: positivism and interpretivism.

Oliver, P. (2010) *The Student's Guide to Research Ethics*. 2nd ed. Maidenhead: Open University Press.
A comprehensive and very useful introduction to research ethics. It includes examples of ethical dilemmas faced when doing research.

Pring, R. (2004) *Philosophy of Educational Research*. 2nd ed. London: Continuum.
This is a thoughtful (and very readable) philosophical discussion about educational research, which will deepen your understanding of the issues involved.

 EPPI-Centre: http://eppi.ioe.ac.uk

The website of the Evidence for Policy and Practice Information and Co-ordinating Centre, part of the Social Science Research Unit at the Institute of Education, University of London. This site has systematic reviews on all aspects of education, providing an overview of many different kinds of research.

2 The process of doing research

What will you learn from this chapter?

This chapter gives you an overview of the whole research process: planning, doing, analysing and writing up. We examine how you can make the most of formal taught sessions, tutorials, online resources and a 'research log'. Also in this chapter, I start to use case studies to illustrate responses to some of the issues you might face as a researcher. By the end of the chapter, you will have a greater understanding of what doing your own project is likely to involve.

Your project

We mentioned in Chapter 1 that research is a planned and structured process. Let us now consider each step in turn.

1. Planning

Planning your research is crucial to success. The better your plan, the better your investigation will be, so be ready to spend time and effort on this.

Your planning involves several elements:

a **Choose a topic:** You consider your experience, interests and understanding, and do some reading in order to identify what you consider to be an important and useful issue to research. We look closely at this process in Chapter 4.

b **Formulate research questions:** Reading further, you construct the research questions which you want your investigation to answer. Chapter 5 examines this important process.

c **Examine what is known already**: You find out what others have written about your topic or what other research has been done on similar themes. This enables you to write your 'literature review'. Chapter 6 deals with this aspect of your project.

d **Design your investigation**: You formulate your 'research design' – the plan of how you will investigate your topic. For this you:

- choose suitable methods of investigation, for instance questionnaires, interviews or observations, and decide who to involve as participants – see Chapter 7

- design your 'data-collection instruments', for instance interview questions or a questionnaire, considered in Chapter 8

- refine these methods so you can trust the data they produce. This relates to 'validity' and 'reliability' which we cover in Chapter 9.

e **Get ethical approval**: Finally, you seek ethical approval so you can begin your investigation. This process is considered in Chapter 9.

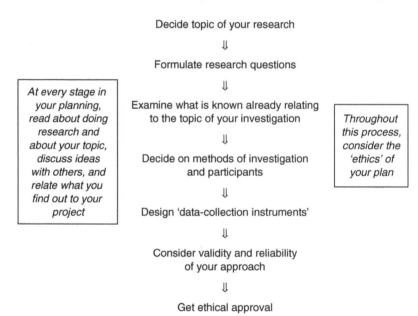

Decide topic of your research

⇓

Formulate research questions

⇓

At every stage in your planning, read about doing research and about your topic, discuss ideas with others, and relate what you find out to your project

Examine what is known already relating to the topic of your investigation

⇓

Throughout this process, consider the 'ethics' of your plan

Decide on methods of investigation and participants

⇓

Design 'data-collection instruments'

⇓

Consider validity and reliability of your approach

⇓

Get ethical approval

Figure 2.1   The planning process

Figure 2.1 shows an outline of the planning process as a whole. Only the main steps are shown – throughout you will also be:

- reading about how to do research
- reading about your topic and associated themes
- discussing ideas with colleagues and your project tutor

- thinking, reflecting, making decisions (and sometimes changing your mind)
- considering the ethics of your plan, so that no one is caused harm or disadvantage as a result of your research.

It is possible that you will be required as part of your course to submit a written outline or 'research proposal', showing the nature of your project and investigation. In most cases, the information you provide will correspond with the steps shown here.

Obstacles

Figure 2.1 gives the impression that this planning process is clear and relatively straightforward. If only it were so. In fact, as your project develops, you are likely to face many problems and constraints. Here are some you may encounter:

- You find that you are not really clear in your own mind what you are investigating. You thought it was clear, then suddenly you are not so sure...
- You realize that the methods you thought you would use will not give you the data you need to answer your research questions.
- You find that the participants you planned to involve are not available, or do not wish to take part.
- You find that the timescale you planned is unrealistic.
- You realize that what you are planning will cause disadvantage to your participants – for instance, the students you planned to involve are revising hard for examinations and should not be interrupted by getting involved in your research at this stage.

Problems like these are one reason why you should take time to plan carefully. You should also be flexible – do not presume that you can fix everything at the start, then stick with it through thick and thin.

 Key Points

During your investigation, you should return many times to your planning – reviewing and reflecting on what you initially intended to do. Be prepared to change, extend or cut back your original ideas. This is not a sign of failure, but part of good research. It makes it more likely that your project will be relevant, useful and carried out in ethical ways.

2. Doing

You have chosen a topic, worked out some questions you wish to answer and have a reasonable plan for collecting data to answer them. Now is the time to 'do' your research. It is a big step to take: you must leave your books, library table and computer, for a while at least, and get into 'the rough ground of practice' (Schwandt, 2003: 362). There are several aspects to this:

a **Contact research 'venue'**: You approach the centre, school, college or other educational setting where you would like to do your research (we consider how to do this in Chapter 10). Note that in some circumstances, in particular with venues linked to health or social services, access to a venue may involve undergoing a criminal records check before doing your research, even if you already have one from your place of study.

b **Get permission**: You get consent from the venue and from individual participants to carry out your research (this ethical issue is dealt with in Chapter 9).

c **Test your methods**: You test your methods and data-collection instruments to find out if and how they need changing before you use them properly (this is called 'piloting' and is also part of Chapter 9).

d **Carry out your investigation**: You undertake your investigation, collecting data and keeping a careful record of what you find out (Chapter 10).

e **Consider ethics**: Once again, throughout this process (and in the further stages below) you act to ensure that no harm or disadvantage is caused by your research.

Figure 2.2 shows this 'doing' part of the research process.

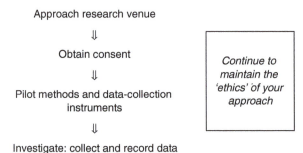

Approach research venue

⇓

Obtain consent

⇓

Pilot methods and data-collection instruments

⇓

Investigate: collect and record data

Continue to maintain the 'ethics' of your approach

Figure 2.2 The 'doing' process

3. Analysing

You have carried out your investigation and collected your data. Now you need to analyse these data in order to generate findings – the answers to your research questions. You will then examine carefully what you find out and finally make recommendations relevant to the topic of your research (see Chapter 11). These recommendations help you and others involved in education to learn from your work and enhance understanding and practice. This process is shown in Figure 2.3.

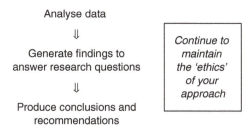

Figure 2.3   The process of analysis

4. Writing up

Research is only really useful if it is shared. You do this by 'writing up' your project, so that others can read, evaluate and learn from what you did and what you found out. We look at this process in detail in Chapter 12.

In reality, you should not leave this part of the research process until you have done everything else. It is much better to jot, scribble and write as you go along, testing out your writing skills with draft text and getting a feel for how your project will look at the end (back up electronic writing too, in case you lose it). Gray (2009: 523–524) summed this up: 'The more time you can devote to writing sections and chapters of the report during the research process itself, the better'. The Project Sheets in this book (Appendix I) will help you with this.

 Key Points

Read and write as your project develops. Reading means that you learn from others, both about your topic and about how to do research. Making notes, using the Project Sheets in this book and composing draft text will give you practice in expressing your ideas and provide material which you can later refine for your final written project.

If you are doing a course, you may have completed several written assignments already. Your research project is likely to be different from these. For your project you will probably be given a clear and definite structure to follow. This structure may vary, but it will probably include similar sections to those presented here:

- **Abstract**: a very short summary of your project: its topic, methods and outcomes
- **Contents**: a list of the contents of your project with page numbers
- **Research issue**: a short summary of your topic, perhaps with clarification of key terminology
- **Justification**: reasons why you chose the topic
- **Research questions**: your research questions
- **Literature review**: an analysis of published literature, discussing what is known already about your topic
- **Methodology**: an analysis of the methods you used, discussing and justifying each one
- **Validity and reliability**: an explanation of how you strengthened the trustworthiness of the data you collected
- **Ethics**: an explanation of how you made sure that your study did not cause harm or disadvantage
- **Presentation and analysis of data**: a close scrutiny of data gathered from your investigation
- **Discussion of findings**: what you found out from these data
- **Conclusions and recommendations**: a summary of findings and a listing of recommendations for practice or for further research, generated by your investigation
- **References**: a complete, accurate list of the references you have used in your text
- **Appendices**: the materials you used in your research. These could include a sample questionnaire, interview questions and your application for ethical approval.

When your written project is almost complete, you should check that it is clear and fully accurate (i.e. proofread it), put together the final version and submit it for marking or for publication. Figure 2.4 shows this process of 'writing up'.

If any sections in this structure seem unclear, do not worry. For now, you only need a 'feel' for the project as a whole. This book will cover each aspect of your research in detail, step by step, and in the last chapter will look more closely at how your whole project is written and put together.

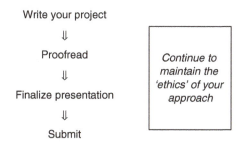

Figure 2.4   The writing-up process

Doing your project well

To do your project well, you need to take full advantage of all the opportunities for study, tuition and discussion open to you. This includes these important aspects:

- understanding your prior experience of research
- working independently
- using online and other resources
- learning from formal sessions
- working with your project tutor
- keeping a 'research log'
- starting to write.

We will now deal with each in turn.

Understanding your prior experience of research

In the previous chapter, I suggested that doing a research project can be challenging, rather scary perhaps. Even experienced researchers are not immune from this feeling. If this is so, it is worth spending a little time early on (on your own, with colleagues or your project tutor) thinking about experiences which you have already had in this area. For instance, in your everyday life, have you ever:

- Filled in a questionnaire or been asked about your opinions face to face?
- Watched something closely to try and understand it better?
- Studied a document carefully (for example, a bus timetable or legal document) to try and find out some specific information from it?

In education, have you ever:

- Been asked your opinion of a teaching approach or educational materials?
- Examined the results of students' tests and tried to see whether they have made progress over time?
- Observed a child or student closely to try and work out what 'makes them tick'?

If the answer to any of these is 'yes' (and I am sure it will be), then you already have some informal, but valuable experiences relating to research. These give you a useful basis from which to move on to more formal project work.

 Activity 2.1   Assessing your prior experience of research

With colleagues identify and discuss your previous experience of the kind listed above. How might this experience act as a baseline for further development of your understanding as you work on your project?

Working independently

'No one can do the research for you; the responsibility is yours and yours alone' (Hart, 1998: viii). It is important that you approach this independence in the right way. Basically you should not expect others to feed information to you – you should go out and seek it yourself. Here is some guidance to help you with this:

- Start work on your project early in your course – research cannot be done in a rush.
- Plan the progress of your work and take responsibility for making it happen.
- Designate regular, substantial time for this in your personal timetable, then stick to this timetable.
- Use this time to read, take notes, prepare, think, investigate, analyse and write.
- Set targets for your progress – keep to them as much as you can, but if you fall behind, make special efforts to catch up.
- At regular intervals, ask your project tutor for face-to-face tutorials and prepare well for these (see below).

- Be aware that in doing research, you also rely on others, for instance on staff and students who will participate, and on your project tutor for advice and guidance. Do not expect them to be available at short notice simply because you have not prepared well in advance. Give them time to respond to your requests and queries.
- Be ready for hiccups, setbacks and obstacles. Give yourself time to deal with these too.

Using online and other resources

Part of this independent learning is to make use of course-related resources. These may be available to you online on a course intranet. They might include materials from taught sessions, a 'Frequently Asked Questions' facility or an online forum. If these are available, you should use them, firstly to get guidance about your project, but also, by contributing to online discussion, to test out your ideas.

Learning from formal sessions

You may also have formal taught sessions with fellow students. These may be part of a 'research methods' module or occasional sessions for the project itself. It is important to use such sessions to gain understanding of your project and how to improve it. Before each session, collect relevant material and do preparatory reading around the topic to be covered. At sessions, take notes of what is said and discussed; ask questions and contribute to discussions – again this will help you to test your ideas against the reactions and experiences of others. After each session, compare notes and ideas with friends and do further reading to consolidate and extend your understanding.

Working with your project tutor

I have already mentioned your 'project tutor' several times (you may know them as your 'supervising tutor' or 'supervisor'). This person is usually a university or college lecturer who has experience in doing research. Their role will vary, but it is likely that she or he will do some or all of the following:

- discuss your project with you at regular intervals
- offer advice and guidance as you progress, and highlight aspects which require attention
- challenge your thinking, so you scrutinize more closely your ideas and their implications
- discuss ethical issues and give you ethical approval to carry out your investigation

- encourage you to set targets for continuing work, for instance to carry out a set of interviews within a certain period of time
- suggest useful sources and materials to inform your thinking
- give feedback on plans, materials and examples of draft text you have produced.

To make the most of this, it is worth thinking about how you will work with your project tutor. Here is my advice:

- **Take the initiative**: For instance, do not wait for your tutor to contact you – you should decide when you need to talk.
- **Prepare for tutorials**: Think about what you want to discuss and questions you want to ask. Take plans, materials or sample text with you as a basis for your discussion.
- **Take notes**: Write down what you discuss, what advice is given and what you need to do next (you could do this as part of your research log – see below).
- **Keep planning ahead**: When you have one tutorial, arrange a date for the next.
- **Keep in contact**: Email between tutorials to keep your tutor informed of your progress and to discuss smaller issues.

 Lauren makes first contact with her tutor

Lauren has been allocated a project tutor and decides to introduce herself. She drafts a brief email: not too formal, but clear and accurate in its composition. She expects that the tutor will appreciate knowing a little about her in advance, and she can take the opportunity to request a first tutorial. Here is Lauren's email:

Mike,

I understand that you are my tutor for my final-year research project. I am looking forward to doing this project, although I must admit that I am a little nervous and unclear about what it might involve.

At this stage I do not know what to investigate. My main interest is in the language development of young children, so this could be a possible area, although I have others in mind too.

I would very much like to discuss my ideas with you at a face-to-face tutorial. Please let me know when this might be possible.

Lauren

Final-year BA student

Keeping a 'research log'

Several times so far we have mentioned taking notes of your thoughts and ideas. Many of these will spring up in your mind as you plan, do, analyse and write up your research. Writing them down is an important part of the reflective process which is a basis to your work. For this I suggest that you maintain a 'research log', a simple record of thoughts, impressions and ideas as you undertake your project:

- You use it to record and explore the decisions you take as you plan and carry out your research.
- You also use it to explore the obstacles you encounter and your deliberations about how to overcome them.
- The log is for you, not for anyone else (even your project tutor need not see it).
- You can use abbreviations, signs and symbols – anything which means something to you. For instance, an asterisk (*) can indicate that there is something you need to do: a reference to find, or an issue to discuss at your next tutorial.
- Your log can be handwritten or kept on your computer; you can add writing to it whenever you wish.

You will find that a research log allows you to capture ideas before they disappear (as they will) into the ether. You can move on to other things and return to them later with a clearer mind. You may find that you can use some of the ideas when writing up your project, particularly when considering problems you faced, justifying decisions you made or exploring conclusions arising from your investigation.

 Ryan explores his thinking in his research log

Ryan has a few concerns about the choice of topic for his research. He decides to unburden and explore these in his research log:

26.10.12

Why have I chosen this topic? It seems relevant generally, but why is it particularly relevant to me? When I was on placement in school, it was identified as something I needed to find out about in greater depth. That seems one good reason for choosing it for my project, at least. *Discuss with tutor.

(Continued)

(Continued)

29.10.12

How can I investigate this topic? Teachers will have a lot to say about it, I am sure, the curriculum coordinator in particular. But so will learning support assistants who work with these students. What about the students themselves? Could they do a questionnaire for me, or maybe a group discussion would be better? *Raise issue on online forum? *Read up on benefits and disadvantages of both, so I can decide.

Starting to write

You can even use your research log (as well as the Project Sheets in this book) to write draft text as you progress. What you write does not have to be perfect – you can revisit these drafts and gradually improve them. We consider the final stages of this ongoing writing process in Chapter 12.

Give it a try

That, then, is the process of research and your approach to doing it. Soon we will start to work through this process step by step. First, however, you have the option in the next chapter of testing your new understanding by examining a piece of published research and analysing the various aspects which we have mentioned so far. I suggest you give it a try.

Further reading 📖

Coles, A. and McGrath, J. (2010) *Your Education Research Project Handbook.* Harlow: Pearson.
This book's unusual approach will not be to everyone's taste, but it provides an alternative view on how research can be structured (page 186) and shows clearly how careful use of tutorials can guide you through your project as a whole.

Cottrell, S. (2008) *The Study Skills Handbook.* 3rd ed. Basingstoke: Palgrave MacMillan.
A substantial handbook with much user-friendly advice on how to manage your time, develop investigative ability, use online learning and many other skills relating to your project.

Naughton, G.M., Rolfe, S.A. and Siraj-Blatchford, I. (2010) *Doing Early Childhood Research: International Perspectives on Theory and Practice.* 2nd ed. Maidenhead: Open University Press.
Writer-researchers from Australia, New Zealand, Portugal and the UK closely examine the research process in the context of early years education.

3   Learning from other research

What will I learn from this chapter?

The previous chapter provided an overview of the research process as a whole. If you studied this carefully, you may already feel confident enough to embark on your own project. If so, you could omit this chapter and move on to Chapter 4. If not, you will find it very useful to undertake the task here. Examining a research project which has already been completed and published will further strengthen your understanding of how to approach your own.

The task

Here is the task for this chapter, followed by a more detailed explanation of each stage.

Project Sheet 1   Learning from other research

Working alone or with colleagues:

1 Find an example of published research relating to education.

2 Read it carefully, annotating the text.

3 Answer these questions, using Project Sheet 1 in Appendix I:

   a What is the main topic of this research? Why was this topic worth investigating?

   b What specific questions did the research try to answer?

(Continued)

(Continued)

    c What published material ('literature') has been used to provide the background or context to the topic being researched?

    d What methods were used to collect data? Who were involved as participants?

    e What does this research report say about validity, reliability and ethics?

    f How were data analysed? What findings were produced?

    g How might these findings inform the development of educational provision, teaching and students' learning?

1. Find an example of published research relating to education

The first step then is to find a suitable piece of published research. We can call this a research 'paper', 'article', 'report' or 'study' – they all mean roughly the same.

What kind of research should I find?

You should find a paper which is:

- **about education**: this is your field and the context of your own project
- **about a research investigation**: many articles are published about education but many do not report on a specific research project. Instead, they may describe an author's experiences, opinions or recommendations for practice. These are not what you need. You want something which describes a specific investigation, carried out in a formal way by the article's author or authors (research is often undertaken by a group of researchers)
- **complete**: it should include consideration of most or all stages of the research process: description of topic, literature, methodology, through to presentation of findings and conclusions, as was described in Chapter 2 and as you will do in your own project
- **at the right level**: published research papers are sometimes lengthy and difficult to read. Others are more accessible. Below I give examples of journals which publish papers at various levels, so you can choose one which matches your interests, experience and understanding.

Where and how can I find it?

The easiest way to find a relevant research paper is to search in research journals. There is a wide range available. Most have a particular theme: a curricular subject, for instance, or a generic issue such as assessment or the use of technology. Most are published in both printed and online formats:

- **Printed format**: your education library may prominently display current issues; past issues may be bound and shelved elsewhere. The library's catalogue will list which printed journals are stocked and which issues are available.

- **Online format**: your education library will also subscribe to online journals, as well as or instead of the printed version. The simplest way to get access to these is to ask at your library. Staff will show you how to 'do a search' for articles about a chosen theme. If you wish to search independently, jump to Chapter 6, which gives more substantial guidance on this process.

Useful journals for this task

Here are some journals with research reports which could be useful for this task:

- *Education 3–13*
- *Support for Learning*
- *Improving Schools*

You will also find some useful papers on websites such as these:

- National Foundation for Educational Research (NFER): www.nfer.ac. uk and its online archive (free to download) of the journal, 'Practical Research for Education' up to 2011: www.pre-online.co.uk
- CERUKplus: www.ceruk.ac.uk, another free online database of education and children's services research in the UK, completed or being undertaken up to the year 2011 (as with many online collections, it is sadly no longer being updated)
- Teaching and Learning Research Programme: www.tlrp.org
- Department for Education: www.education.gov.uk/research

If you would like something rather more challenging, try these journals:

- *British Educational Research Journal*
- *Educational Action Research*
- *Oxford Review of Education*

If you have a specialist area, you could try a journal related to that area, for example:

- *Journal of Early Childhood Research*
- *Research in Post-Compulsory Education*
- *Journal of Computer Assisted Learning*
- *Research in Mathematics Education*

2. Read your chosen research article carefully, annotating the text

Print out or photocopy the research paper you have selected, or download it to your computer, as long as copyright regulations allow (check with your library or at the website of the Copyright Licensing Agency: www.cla. co.uk). Using Project Sheet 1, first make a careful note of the details of the paper, so you can reference it (see Chapter 12 for more discussion on this).

Now look through the text, making initial rough notes about the research and what it found out, and highlighting sections of particular interest. Then decide how you will go about answering each question in the task in turn. If you are working with others, you could allocate particular questions to each member of the group, or everyone could work on every question and then pool answers.

3. Answer the questions

Make notes relevant to each question on Project Sheet 1. It may not be easy to answer them all. For instance, the research questions (Question 3b) may not be clearly listed, or there may be no mention at all of ethics (Question 3e). If this is the case, try to see if there are less obvious ways in which the paper considers these elements. For instance, research questions may be described rather than listed, and there may be mention of safeguards for participants, even though the word 'ethics' is not used.

When you have answered all the questions as best you can, you can extend the task a step further. Prepare a 5- or 10-minute presentation about the research paper for your course colleagues. Again, if you are working in a group, share this responsibility amongst you. In addition, tackle this extra question as well:

(h)   What is my/our opinion of this research? What are its strengths and weaknesses? What criticisms do I/we have of the investigation? How might it have been improved?

This extra question gives you an opportunity to be analytical and constructively critical, and to evaluate the value of a research study for yourself and for others in education. Section 2 of Taber (2007), with its advice on how to evaluate critically the quality and relevance of research reports in relation to educational practice, will help you with this task. Doing a presentation will also give you valuable experience of summarizing and appraising research for a wider audience – these are useful skills to develop for your own project.

Case study

Rebecca and Josh are preparing to undertake their own projects and decide to do the task in this chapter in order to get a better understanding of how research is carried out and written up. The case study which follows shows how they approach and complete this task.

 Rebecca and Josh do their task

Rebecca and Josh are both interested in the role of assessment in education. With the help of their university library, they look in printed journals and online for published papers on the topic and find this:

Elder, A.D. (2010) 'Children's self-assessment of their school work in elementary school', *Education 3–13*, 38(1): 5–11.

Having looked it through, they decide that this would be a good article to use for this task. They then divide the task between them: Rebecca will look for the paper's research questions, the methods used and mention of validity, reliability and ethics; Josh will examine the paper's findings and consider how these relate to educational practice. They use Project Sheet 1 for their notes. Figure 3.1 shows the ideas which they put together.

a	What is the main topic of this research? Why was this topic worth investigating?

This research was carried out in the USA. The main topic is the way in which children reflect on their learning and self-assess their work in school. The authors usefully define 'self-assessment' as 'the process by which students come to gauge their level of performance and understanding' (page 5).

Elder calls self-assessment 'a critical step for children to become self-regulated learners' (page 5). She claims that there has been little research on children's assessment relative to specific academic tasks.

(Continued)

(Continued)

We think the paper could help educators to understand better the practical application of assessment in schools, in particular the way in which children themselves can monitor their learning.

b   What specific questions did the research try to answer?

The article states three questions which were the focus of the research:

1. From what sources do children gather information about their progress?

2. What sorts of criteria or standards do students use in evaluating themselves?

3. How does self-assessment change with age and schooling?

c   What published material ('literature') has been used to provide the background or context to the topic being researched?

Elder writes about several pieces of literature which highlight the importance of self-assessment. She mentions other literature which suggests that students' self-assessments are often inaccurate or demonstrate over-confidence.

d   What methods were used to collect data? Who were involved as participants?

The research interviewed two groups: the first had 17 children aged 6 and 7 (10 girls and 7 boys); the other had 20 children aged 10 and 11 (10 girls and 10 boys). These children came from three classrooms in a public elementary school in the USA. The classrooms were recommended by the principal as having teachers who 'engaged students in reflective thought' (page 6) and where some form of self-appraisal was practised. The interviews were carried out individually, each lasting about 30 minutes. There were four open-ended questions and 24 items using a scale (called a 'Likert scale') which asked the children to rate their self-assessment in school.

e   What does this research report say about validity, reliability and ethics?

There is no mention of any of these words, however:

   o *The author mentions that there was 'early pilot testing' (page 6) of the Likert scale items with other students. Is this part of validity and reliability – trialling questions and improving them before using them properly?*

   o *All children in the three classes were asked to participate and only those who agreed and whose parents also agreed took part. We think that this idea of agreeing to take part could be part of ethics.*

f   How were data analysed? What findings were produced?

The researcher 'coded' the open-ended responses and then divided them again according to certain themes. She then counted the frequencies with which these themes were mentioned, or highlighted in the Likert-scale items. She used something called the 'Fisher's Exact test' to check the links between children's developmental levels and what they said they used for self-assessment. Tables of figures from this test are presented in the paper, although we had difficulty understanding what some of these meant. The findings are clearer: Elder concludes that as children get older, they 'are amassing a variety of ways to evaluate their work that includes varied sources' (page 10).

g   How might these findings inform the development of educational provision, teaching and students' learning?

We agree with the author that it is important to understand the sources and criteria which children use when they evaluate their own work. That way we can guide them to new ways of doing this if it is helpful. As students get older and do more independent work, it is important that they get better at appraising what they do. As the author writes: 'By helping students reflect on themselves and their accomplishments, teachers can help students invest effort, interpret their progress, promote the internalization of academic standards, and gain a sense of self-efficacy' (page 10).

Figure 3.1   Rebecca and Josh do their task

Finally, in preparation for a presentation to colleagues, Rebecca and Josh discuss the article as a whole. Figure 3.2 shows their evaluation of its strengths and weaknesses.

h   What is our opinion of this research? What are its strengths and weaknesses? What criticisms do we have of the investigation? How might it have been improved?

We had not really thought much before about how students self-assess their work, just that we have seen teachers encouraging them to do this. This article got us discussing the strategies which children use and how these relate to their age. Elder writes in a clear and concise way, but we would have liked more explanation of the test which she used to examine links between children's developmental levels and their ways of self-assessment. Also, it would be useful to know what changes she made to her Likert scale as a result of the pilot testing she mentions. We would like to know how to 'code' answers – might we be doing that in our own project? Finally, we noticed that interviews with the children were carried out individually – we are not sure if this would be a good way for us to carry out our own research.

Figure 3.2   Rebecca and Josh critically evaluate their chosen article

And now to your own project...

Doing this task will have strengthened your understanding of educational research and the steps involved in doing your own project. You are now ready to take these steps. The first is to identify a topic for your research. Surprisingly this is not always easy to do, but very important for your project as a whole. We deal with this initial process in the next chapter.

SECTION TWO

Doing Research

4 Choosing your topic

What will I learn from this chapter?

Chapter 4 considers the first step in the process described in Chapter 2: choosing a topic for your project. If you have not done this yet, it will help you do so; if you have, then it will allow you to evaluate and refine your choice. A four-stage process is presented, the last showing how to sharpen the focus of your investigation so you can scrutinize an area in depth rather than superficially in breadth, and thereby produce a study of value for yourself and for others.

Choosing a topic

Education is so rich and varied you would think that it would be fairly easy to choose just one aspect for investigation. If only it were so. You may not be sure what is worthy of research, or wonder what (with so much written already) there is left to investigate. You may have a general area in mind, but be unsure how to pinpoint a specific aspect for close scrutiny. This first decision may not therefore be straightforward. However, make it you must, and the sooner you do so, the easier and more focused your further work will be.

Examined below are four stages for deciding on a suitable topic for your study. These are:

1 Thinking about education
2 Investigating further
3 Justifying your choice
4 Narrowing down

1. Thinking about education

We start in a general way, by thinking in broad terms about what education consists of and the various areas which might deserve investigation. Here is my list and some questions associated with each:

Policy and practice: Education is to a large extent planned in advance. It is set out in policy documentation, put together by national or local government and by nurseries, schools and colleges. Yet in practice much educational activity is spontaneous, especially in busy classrooms. *What educational policy is there? What does it say? To what extent is policy evident, or not evident, in everyday classroom practice?*

Curriculum: Curriculum is what is taught and learnt, as part of formal design or informal activity. A curriculum usually has 'subjects', such as mathematics and geography, although how these are categorized and organized varies according to students' age, educational setting and cultural context. *What can a curriculum look like? To what extent is it broad and balanced? Which subjects have priority and how is this evident in classroom activity and learning?*

Organization: Educational institutions have phases, departments, year groups, classes and timetables. Routines often abound: taking an attendance register, moving between lessons, starting and ending the day. There are leadership structures amongst staff (and sometimes amongst students too), rules for behaviour and detailed procedures for safety, use of volunteers and many other elements. *How is an educational institution organized? What procedures help it to run smoothly? How does the way a setting is structured help (or not help) students to study, learn and prepare themselves for an independent future?*

Teaching: Teaching is done in many different ways: talking from the front, organizing group activity, or working with individuals. Teachers may encourage students to sit and listen, re-enact situations, use resources or carry out experiments. A teacher may work alone or with others. *What kinds of teaching approaches are there? How might different approaches lead to different kinds of learning and achievement?*

Learning: Children and students are varied too: boys and girls, older and younger, rapid learners and those who advance with greater difficulty. They vary in mood and attitude: keen or reluctant, withdrawn or outgoing. Yet there are many similarities too: attitudes, emotions, maturational needs, and the ways in which they learn. *What are the similarities and differences amongst students? What do they gain from varied opportunities for learning?*

Wider development: Education is not just about formal learning – social and emotional development is part of it too. 'Ethos' is important – the values and beliefs which underlie the daily work of an educational setting and how these translate into the behaviour of staff, students and their families. *What contributes to the ethos of an educational establishment? How is it evident? How is social and emotional development enhanced by these values and beliefs?*

 Activity 4.1   Collecting ideas about education

1 Choose one area listed above.
2 Discuss with colleagues the questions relating to that area.
3 Identify in your discussion aspects of education which might deserve closer examination and which could form a general theme for your research.

2. Investigating further

You now have a rough and ready list of possible broad areas of investigation. Much research, however, addresses issues where there is tension, debate or 'unresolved controversy' – a 'riddle that seeks a solution' (Walliman, 2011: 29). To incorporate this element in your own research, you need to be aware of current issues being discussed in education. Here are ways you can achieve this:

- Scan the quality newspapers and other media for news and comment about current issues.
- Quick-read a couple of recently published books or journal articles about education to see what issues are examined, or (even better) which are recommended 'for further research'.
- Listen to teachers and other professionals – what are they talking about? What are parents and students talking about? Listen to them too. What ideas are being suggested for changing and improving educational practice?
- Use what you learn to refine and adapt your idea for your research topic.

 Lucy gets interested in government policy on behaviour

Lucy did Activity 4.1 with her colleagues. They discussed 'policy' in general and the importance of policy for behaviour

(Continued)

(Continued)

management in schools in particular. That night Lucy watches a television programme on that issue, with a government official, headteacher and school student in heated debate. Lucy is not sure who is right, but from the TV argument and her earlier discussion she concludes that the topic could and should be explored further.

She starts to ask herself some questions: What behaviour management policies are used in my local school? To what extent does the school's practice match government recommendations? What do staff, students and parents feel about what happens and how it could be changed? My research project in the making, she thinks, and resolves to work further on this possibility.

Over the next few days, Lucy uses library and Internet resources to develop her idea. In an education newspaper, she finds a leader comment which questions government plans in this area. In an education journal, she finds an article which considers the extent to which schools, parents or students themselves should take responsibility for improving student behaviour. She chats with a couple of friends and they start to argue about this 'responsibility' debate in particular. Lucy is encouraged by all of this: the variety of opinion and general uncertainty seem to indicate fertile ground for an investigation of her own.

 Project Sheet 2   Research topic (first question)

You may have done the first Project Sheet as part of the previous chapter. Completing these Sheets will help you to build up a framework for your project as you progress. If you now have a general project topic in mind, make a note of it against Question a) on Project Sheet 2 (in Appendix I).

3. Justifying your choice

Stage 3 of choosing a topic involves considering your reasons for choosing this topic. We now consider some options you have for this, with case-study examples.

International: The first option is the broadest of all. Is the topic you are investigating an area of international concern? Is it discussed in international education journals, such as the *International Journal of Inclusive Education* or *European Journal of Education?*

National: Closer to home, is your topic an area of concern in your own country? Is it discussed by government, educators or even the general public? Does it relate to curriculum or social developments specific to your country?

Local: Is this an issue which education professionals in your locality (or even at your anticipated research venue) wish to understand better, or address in their own practice?

 Jessica and parental involvement

Jess has seen discussion in government literature about professional and parental cooperation in early years education. She also knows that most nurseries in her area wish to strengthen this aspect of their work. Perhaps her research could – even in a small way – contribute to national understanding on this topic, as well as guiding development at the school where she might do her research. She decides to find out if there is also international interest in this topic, which might justify her choice even further.

Professional: This area of justification relates more to your own needs as a developing professional. Will your investigation help you to do your job better or advance your career, or both? If you are on a course which involves working towards competency standards, for instance teacher training, could it provide evidence towards one or more of the standards which relate to your topic?

 Richard's career

Richard is a teacher of English, seeking to further his career. He decides that investigating how standards of English can be promoted across the curriculum will help him to improve his understanding and be beneficial when taking on departmental or whole-school responsibility in the future.

Personal: Lastly, your own interests can provide relevant personal justification for choosing a particular topic. Note that interest is not the same as expertise, so the topic could be an area which you do not know much about. Indeed, this may mean you are more curious and questioning when you carry out your research.

Raj's interest in IT

Raj has a strong personal interest in information technology, and wishes to extend this interest to his work in education. He would like in particular to discover how mobile-phone technology could be used by further-education teachers to enhance students' learning. Raj's interest is a meaningful personal justification for his choice of topic.

Key Points

A well-justified topic is one which:

- will contribute to local, national or even international understanding
- will be useful for your own professional development
- you are interested in (even if you do not know a great deal about it).

Project Sheet 2   Research topic (contd.)

Consider possible justifications for your topic and complete the relevant sections of Project Sheet 2 in Appendix I.

4. Narrowing down

The final stage of choosing a topic is to sharpen the focus of your choice, so you can investigate a precise issue in depth. If your topic is still rather broad, here are ways to narrow it down, with an example for each:

- **Focus on one area of curriculum**: for instance, if your topic is the role of teaching assistants in primary education, you could investigate their specific responsibilities in relation to the teaching of physical education.

- **Investigate an aspect of curriculum delivery**: if your interest is in mathematics, you could focus on fractions and the ways they are explained.

- **Examine a teaching approach**: if you wish to investigate the education of high-achieving students, you could examine a particular teaching strategy, for instance the involvement of experts in their curriculum, or use of a particular resource, such as GIS systems in geography.

- **Choose a way of learning**: if you are interested in ways of learning, you could choose to investigate one of these, for instance how students use work experience to increase knowledge and understanding.

- **Choose an aspect of activity**: for example, if you want to research children's activity in an early years setting, you could choose to examine ways in which room layout can promote their independence.

- **Choose an age group**: if you are investigating the use of artefacts in the teaching of history, you could, for instance, choose to focus on classes of students aged 11 and 12.

- **Choose a group**: if you wish to research the teaching of writing, you could choose to explore approaches for children for whom English is not a first language.

- **Make a comparison**: if you want to explore the topic: 'What is the value of education?', you could decide to compare the perspectives of students and staff.

To get a really sharp focus to your study, you could combine any of the examples above as your project develops, as Lucy does here:

 Lucy finds her focus

Earlier, we left Lucy developing her project about behaviour management in an interesting way. As her reading and thinking continue, she sharpens its focus further. She decides to do this in two ways:

- She decides to focus on one aspect of her 'responsibility' theme: students' self-responsibility for their behaviour and how this can be promoted within school.

(Continued)

(Continued)

- She decides to specify the age of students she will investigate: 11 to 14, as this is the age range about which a recent official report is most concerned.

Lucy has now determined the topic of her project: 'Promoting self-responsibility for behaviour amongst young secondary-school students'. She knows that she may need to adapt or refine this further (and there is further guidance below which she should take note of), but for now she is confident with the stage she has reached.

Project Sheet 2   Research topic (final question)

By finding your focus, you can complete Question (g) of Project Sheet 2. Note that nothing is fixed and definite on these Project Sheets – you can change or improve what you write at any stage as you think fit. Research always involves changes in plans and ideas. Your project is no exception and will be stronger as a result.

A warning about 'cause and effect'

Before we move on to some final guidance, we should look again at an important warning from Chapter 1 about the difficulties of looking for cause and effect. I wrote: 'There are simply too many alternative explanations for any "effect" that may be indicated by the investigation'. You may nevertheless have found yourself moving towards this kind of topic when you completed Project Sheet 2. It is worth, therefore, looking in greater depth – through the experiences of Jeffrey this time – at some of the potential pitfalls of this approach and at ways in which you could still, with care, explore something along these lines.

Jeffrey gets into deep water

Jeffrey decides to investigate how students' school attendance affects their learning. He plans to analyse the register to find out how regularly each student attends. He will then look at the results of educational tests they have taken. He will compare one list with another: do students who attend regularly achieve the best results? He is fairly sure he will find that they do. His research will therefore show that regular school attendance (the cause) leads to high levels of achievement (the effect). He goes for a relaxing swim to wind down after a busy day.

In the pool, however, he starts to think...

- Perhaps there are students who *enjoy* learning and *that* is the reason they attend more regularly. So it could be the other way round: successful learning 'causes' regular attendance.

- Perhaps some students have parents who make sure they attend each day. Those parents take a strong interest in their children's education and motivate them to do well. So strong parenting 'causes' both good learning and regular attendance.

Jeffrey starts to see how difficult it is to show that one thing causes another. There is always a range of other possible explanations about what might be causing what. He starts to think again about his project...

In general terms, determining cause and effect is a very important role of research (medical investigations try to do it all the time). However, it takes a long time and requires sophisticated research procedures, often repeated many times, to do well. For a beginner, doing a small-scale project, it is not really an option. Here, for instance, are some topics which you might treat with great caution: 'The effect of the use of drama on children's learning'; 'How does changing the classroom environment affect students' achievement?'; and Jeffrey's initial topic: 'The effect of attendance on students' test results at school'.

Does that mean that you should not look at 'effect' at all? No, it does not. After all, what causes what is important in education. When educators work in a certain way, they believe it will have a beneficial effect: in particular that children or students will learn. However, the complexities of this kind of research mean that you should be very clear about what exactly you are investigating and how in your project you state your intentions and the conclusions you draw. Let us go back to Jeffrey and see how he has redesigned his project.

Jeffrey finds a better way

Jeffrey finishes his swim and the next day goes to talk about his difficulty with his project tutor. As a result of their discussion, he decides that he will not try and 'prove' any cause and effect. Instead, he will use his investigation to collect evidence which may indicate a link or 'relationship' between regular attendance and high achievement, and then assess the strengths and weaknesses of that evidence. For instance:

- He will examine students' achievement results and their attendance and see if there is some kind of 'correlation' between the two: does low achievement in general equate with poor attendance? To what extent does high achievement equate with regular attendance? Jeffrey knows that any conclusions will not prove what is causing what, but they may indicate a relationship of some kind.

- He decides to ask the assessment coordinator and classroom teachers about how they think attendance relates to results. He understands that he will be exploring perspectives and experiences, not trying to pin down actual cause and effect.

- He will also discuss the issue with students themselves: What do they feel helps them to do well in their tests and examinations? To what extent, in their view, is attending school part (or not part) of this? Their perspectives might provide some interesting insights into the issue as a whole.

Using these approaches, Jeffrey will collect some useful indications of the extent to which attendance relates to low or high performance (and possibly ways in which it does not). They will not prove that one thing causes another, but he will make clear in his written project that he does not intend to show that. His purpose, stated in his project plan or proposal, is rather to explore the relationship between attendance and achievement in greater depth.

Further considerations

By now you should have an overall theme for your research and have given it a sharper focus. Before you make a firm decision, however, here are further important questions to check, together with relevant examples:

Course expectations: Is your topic in line with them?

As a student, you will be subject to course expectations and require-ments. You may have a list of 'learning outcomes' to address; or a list of topics from which you must choose; or stipulations about how your investigation should be carried out. Whatever I advise in this book, you should not move away from the requirements of your course, unless you get express permission from your project tutor to do so.

 Heidi's course requirements

Heidi's course documentation stipulates that projects should not involve direct contact with schools during teaching time. Heidi's university feels that if they allowed this, local schools would find their children's learning unduly disrupted. Heidi therefore chooses a topic which she can investigate by examining policy documen-tation and interviewing selected school staff out of teaching time.

Clarity: Is your topic clear to you and to others?

Being very clear about your topic is one of the most important aspects of doing research. It means that you understand what you are investi-gating and that your readers understand it in the same way. If any ele-ment is vague, or open to misinterpretation, you should clarify it as early as possible. If your topic is unfamiliar to readers not as involved in education as you are, try to explain or define it, even at this early stage. Educational jargon, such as 'learning styles', 'personalization', 'active learning', 'creative curriculum' and 'emotional intelligence', will need particular attention. Hart (1998: 121) called this 'placing boundar-ies around the meaning of a term'.

 Clare and 'Thinking Skills'

Clare wishes to investigate the teaching of 'Thinking Skills' in school. However, her boyfriend tells her that he is not certain what 'thinking skills' are. So Clare expands the description of her topic as follows: *'Thinking skills' help children to discover and explore new knowledge and understanding in independent ways. They include the ability to research, to collaborate with others and to evaluate sources of information.* Clare will explore these ways of learning in her project.

Methods: Have you got methods in mind for investigating your topic?

It is worth thinking too about how you might investigate your topic. Look ahead to Chapter 7 to see what kind of approaches are available to you. At this stage, are you reasonably confident that you will be able to use some of these?

 Amy's methods

> Amy's project is about the use of online portfolios in the assessment of college students' learning. She can imagine investigating this topic by giving a questionnaire to students, interviewing lecturers and examining college documentation such as its assessment policy.

Access: Can you get to your research participants?

Most research studies in education involve getting access to an early years setting, school, college or other educational establishment. You may wish to talk to a headteacher, coordinator, teachers, assistants, young children, students or parents. You will be relying on the generosity and interest of such people, taking their time and making use of their experience and expertise. You need to bear this in mind when choosing the topic of your research:

- Will you be able to negotiate access to an educational setting where you can investigate this topic?
- Will people be available for you to talk to?
- Will they be interested in taking part?

You may not know the answers to these questions at this stage, but you should have a general feeling that the answer to them will be 'yes'.

 Matt and traveller children

> Matt's first idea is to research educational services for children from traveller families. This will involve getting access to the local specialist service. However, he knows that this service is

> currently being reorganized and would probably find it difficult to accommodate him. In the circumstances, he decides that a different topic would be more realistic at this time.

Ethics: Are you sure that your topic will not cause harm or upset?

In Chapter 1, we discussed the ethics of research, how your investigation should not cause harm or disadvantage to participants or to yourself. You need to think about this factor when choosing your topic. If in doubt, discuss the issue with your project tutor or look ahead to Chapter 9 where we consider it further.

 Dan's project on race and ethnicity

> Dan has an interest in race and ethnicity, in particular how teenage students perceive these issues. He is aware that this is a sensitive topic which could cause unease or distress if handled badly. What would happen, for instance, if a student made a racist comment during a group interview: what would Dan do? He discusses his intention with his project tutor, who advises him that the topic can be tackled, but should be carefully considered at every stage. The tutor asks Dan to read up on research ethics (for instance, Alderson and Morrow, 2011) and to bring a more detailed plan for discussion at a future tutorial. This plan should show how Dan aims to minimize the possibilities of causing upset or harm to participants, and what he would do if such upset inadvertently occurred.

Practicalities: Is the project do-able?

What seems reasonable at first can become unmanageable as your project progresses. At this stage, and at later stages too, you should ask yourself:

- Will my topic be manageable within the scope of a small-scale investigation?
- Is it do-able within the time frame which I have to complete it?

Manisha's timescale

Manisha wants to investigate how students prepare for formal state examinations. She would compare their perceptions before and after the examinations take place. Manisha realizes, however, that this timescale does not correspond to how her own course is organized. She therefore redesigns her topic to fit in with the timescale she has available.

Originality: Is your topic 'original'?

Finally, here is a rather tricky concept: the 'originality' of your research. The value of your project is increased if it contributes new knowledge and understanding, but with the wealth of research already carried out, you may feel: 'How can I find anything interesting or original to say?'

Do not despair. Here are some ways in which (with careful planning) your research project can have a degree of originality, even on a topic which has already been widely investigated:

- It is likely that no one has researched this topic in the particular educational setting where you will investigate it.
- It is possible to design your investigation in ways not adopted by other researchers.
- It is possible that no other research will reach exactly the same kind of conclusions as your own.

Also remember Stage 4 above, about sharpening the focus of your research. As the scope of your study becomes tighter, you will find that there is less relevant research already available. You may eventually find that what you first thought was well researched is not so well researched after all. Your own investigation therefore becomes a useful addition to the work already carried out.

Jade finds originality

Jade wants to investigate the teaching of young children with dyslexia. She finds that there is already a great deal of research on this topic. However, she discovers that a local school where she might do her research is well regarded locally for its innovative work with parents and carers of these children. A teacher at the school tells her that no one has looked at their work in depth before. Jade decides to focus her study on this aspect and becomes more confident that her project will contribute to wider understanding on home–school links in relation to these children.

 Key Points

Make sure your project topic is understandable, do-able, ethical and in line with course expectations. Try to identify an element of originality so your work can contribute to wider educational knowledge and understanding.

Your title

This brings us finally to the title of your project. There are various ways of composing this and your project tutor may give specific recommendations about its format. Here are four possibilities:

1 **As a statement**: this kind of title is a simple statement of the chosen topic. Here are some examples:

The uses of 'circle time' to strengthen emotional awareness in young children

Increasing understanding of cultural diversity in a secondary school

Perspectives of young adults about opportunities for lifelong learning

2 **As issues to be researched**: using this style, you simply state the issue or issues which will be investigated (perhaps followed after a colon by an explanatory phrase). For example:

Assessment and achievement

Career advice for students with special educational needs

Gender and sport: views of boys and girls about competitive physical activity in school

3 **As a question**: some researchers like to compose their title as a question which is answered by the investigation. For example:

How can design of a school library encourage boys to read?

What role can parents and carers play in promoting the ethos of a school?

How can a college support socially disadvantaged students in their learning?

4 **As a memorable phrase**: you may have noticed that the titles of some journal articles start with a succinct, memorable phrase. One example is Kelly and Saunders (2010), whose paper about leadership starts its title: 'New heads on the block'. Others start with a quotation drawn from data collected during the investigation, such as Read and Hurford (2010), whose title begins: 'I don't know how to read longer novels'. To succeed, this kind of phrase should reflect or summarize accurately the content of your project, and therefore you will not be able to choose it until your research is almost complete.

Project Sheet 3 Topic checklist

As you can see, there is much to think about when choosing a topic. It is the first important decision in the large number of decisions you will make when designing and doing your research. Project Sheet 3 in Appendix I is a checklist of the advice that has been given in this chapter. Use it to monitor your progress, to highlight concerns to be addressed and to draft your first attempt at your project's title.

Ready to progress

Amelia thinks through her choice of topic

Amelia has been deciding on a topic for her dissertation project. In her research log, she reviews her choice and how she will justify it to her project tutor:

I have covered many different aspects of education during my course. One area I find particularly interesting is the teaching of young children with special educational needs and disabilities. But the topic is very large. How can I make it more specific and manageable for my project?

On my school placement last year there were four children with special educational needs. Two needed extra tuition, one had severe language difficulties, the fourth needed special rules to help him follow class routine. Each child had an 'Individual Education Plan' (IEP), which listed some immediate targets for learning, with dates to achieve them by. I noticed that the children themselves were involved in deciding these targets and monitoring their progress towards them, and they seemed to work harder to achieve them as a result. I also know that the official government document, the *SEN Code of Practice* (Department for Education and Skills, 2001), recommends that children should be involved in decisions about their education. I have also read Feiler and Watson (2010), who call for professional collaboration to enable children with learning and communication difficulties to express their views.

I would like to investigate this aspect of education in more detail. So I have decided that my project topic will be: 'How children with special educational needs and disabilities can contribute to their Individual Education Plan'.

I feel that the topic is clear and manageable within the time frame for my project. It has a national importance, as evident in the Code of Practice and other documents, and it is important for me too, because when I work in schools, I want to know how best to involve children in their learning. I think that my placement school from last year will let me carry out my investigation there – it could help them to evaluate their own practice also. I can envisage examining school policy documents and examples of IEPs, observing children in class, and carrying out interviews with teachers, the school's SEN Coordinator, and the children themselves. There will be ethical issues for me to consider, for instance how I talk to children about this topic.

Amelia can now start to plan her project and undertake relevant reading, all with a real sense of purpose and direction. If you have clarified the topic of your research, then you are in the same position. You are ready to progress to a very important element of the planning process: determining the exact questions which your research project will try to answer. That is our next chapter.

Further reading 📖

Blaxter, L., Hughes, C. and Tight, M. (2010) *How to Research*. 4th ed. Maidenhead: Open University Press.
In Chapter 2, 'Getting Started', the authors call choosing your topic 'the single most important decision you have to make in doing research'. Check their suggestions for 'focusing down' what you intend to investigate.

Education 3–13: Journal of the Association for the Study of Primary Education.
This journal analyses practice, research and theory relating to the education of children aged between 3 and 13. Articles are clear and accessible for education students and practitioners, and give plenty of ideas for your own investigation.

Forum: For Promoting 3–19 Comprehensive Education.
This journal offers topical, often forthright analysis of UK government education policy. Contributions are drawn from classroom teachers, as well as from universities and colleges. These are 'opinion pieces', rather than formal research papers, but the areas of debate will help you when identifying a topic for your own project.

Sharp, J. (2009) *Success with Your Education Research Project.* Exeter: Learning Matters.
Chapter 2 asks: 'So where do the topics for individual research projects come from?' and suggests some useful ways of getting your mind working in the right way, such as brainstorming, doodling and drawing up a 'concept map'. A new edition of this book will be published in 2012.

5 Research questions

What will you learn from this chapter?

In this chapter, we explore the idea of 'research questions'. I explain what these are and how they are important for the success of your whole project. You will see how you can design them well and what kind you should avoid. There is a checklist to use while planning and doing your project, so your questions remain clear, understandable and accurate in relation to your study as a whole.

What are research questions?

You may already have a good idea of what research questions are, especially if you did the task in Chapter 3. However, they are so crucial to the success of your project that it is important to take a close look at them at this stage. Here are some definitions of research questions from the literature:

'A breakdown of the working title, splitting it into questions which the research project will seek to tackle' (Basit, 2010: 48).

'[They make] explicit the precise area of an investigation … the specific aspect(s) which is or are of particular interest' (Lewis and Munn, 2004: 5).

'The central focus of your investigation' (Macintyre, 2000: 30).

And here is my definition:

 Key Points

> Research questions are the questions which you seek to answer in your investigation.

My new camera

I have decided to buy a new camera. I want to make sure that I choose the right one. So I ask myself some questions. My main question is: *Which camera shall I buy*? To answer this, I ask myself several smaller ones as well. For example:

- Which camera will take the best pictures?
- Which camera looks the best?
- Which camera offers good value for money?

These are my 'research questions'. To answer them, I need to investigate, for instance, by looking at online reviews or examining cameras in a shop. So what are research questions? *They are the questions which your investigation will try to answer.*

Why do you need research questions?

As we saw in Chapter 1, research is all about finding out things that we did not know before. The trouble is that you could do your research project on all sorts of topics and find out all sorts of new things. So in Chapter 4 we discussed how you can narrow down the focus and therefore explore your topic in depth. Designing clear research questions is the next important way of doing this. When your questions are carefully thought-out, your project will be well defined and manageable, and the reader of your written project will know exactly what it is all about.

When do you decide them?

Lewis and Munn (2004: 5) called research questions 'the vital first steps in any research'. It is best to formulate them soon after you have decided your research topic. Later in this chapter, you will see one way of putting together a first draft.

After that, you will want to keep looking back at what you have written. You could find that as your project progresses you drift away from your initial intentions as expressed in your questions. You may then need either to adapt them so they are relevant again, or change how you are carrying out your investigation. As Lewis and Munn (2004: 14) pointed out: 'It is unlikely that the first set of research questions you produce will be the set you finally use'.

 **Key Points**

> Tweaking and adapting your research questions during planning and investigation is good research practice. Your research questions remain 'provisional' until you present the final text of your written project.

How many do you need?

There is no rule about how many research questions a project should have. Some have a single research question, others have a large number. For an undergraduate research project, I suggest you start with three research questions. My experience is that this is enough to cover various aspects of a topic, but not too many for a relatively small-scale investigation. For a Masters-level project, you might need more than this: perhaps four or five to cover the various aspects of your theme. These may include smaller 'sub-questions' – we will cover this possibility later in the chapter.

Examples

Here are some examples of simple research questions for projects in education:

- What strategies are used in this nursery to encourage children to engage in cooperative play?
- In the views of students, what are the benefits and disadvantages of museum visits for the learning of history?
- How could staff training improve the teaching of basic skills in this college?

What makes 'good' research questions?

 **Key Points**

> It is not easy to write good research questions, but it is surprisingly easy to write bad ones.

Let us start with three characteristics of good research questions which you should try and achieve, with a case study to illustrate each:

1. Clarity

Research questions make transparent what you are trying to find out. If they are not clear, they may indicate that you are not certain about the exact focus of your investigation, and your reader is unlikely to be certain about this either.

When Sarah started thinking about her project, she wrote this research question: *How are children newly arrived from other countries helped to take part in school activities?* As her planning progressed, she started to worry about the term, 'school activities'. Did she mean learning in the classroom, or more social activities, such as lunchtimes and special events? She wanted it to mean the latter, so she adapted her question to clarify this: *How are children newly arrived from other countries helped to take part in social aspects of the school curriculum?*

2. Understandability

Research questions make complete sense to you and to readers of your written project. Moreover, everyone understands them in the same way – there is no ambiguity. If you think your questions mean one thing, and your readers think they mean something different, there will be confusion about what you are trying to investigate.

For his project, Paul wrote this research question: *In the views of teachers, how can use of the library help children's literacy?* However, he found some people thought he was referring to the school library; others presumed it was the local public library. Paul adapted his question so everyone would understand it in the same way: *In the views of teachers, how can use of the local community library help children's literacy?*

3. Accuracy

Your questions describe precisely what you are trying to find out. If they do not do this, there will be a mismatch between your stated intentions and what you actually do in your investigation. Again, your readers will be confused about what you are really trying to accomplish.

Bal had this research question: *What rewards are used to promote cooperative behaviour amongst students in this school?* Bal soon realized that she was investigating not just the use of rewards, but also the use of sanctions, like missing breaktime or detention after school. Her research question was therefore not accurate. She changed it to: *What rewards and sanctions are used to promote cooperative behaviour amongst students in this school?*

Where to start?

You have chosen your topic and sharpened its focus. You are using your reading to inform the choices you have made. Now it is time to write the research questions for your own project.

There is no single way of setting these out – what you ask and how you ask it will depend on what you are trying to find out. As a beginning researcher, however, you may be rather unsure about what to do. So I will now take you carefully through the design of three research questions for a piece of exploratory research. If you are unsure, then I suggest you follow this guidance. If you feel more confident, or if the guidance does not fit your project, then you may want to develop a framework of your own. The section 'Other kinds of research questions', later in this chapter, will help you to do this.

A suggested framework

Research Question 1: Finding out what is happening already

A useful place to start is to find out in depth what is happening already in relation to your topic. For example:

1 You are investigating community involvement in a college. For your first research question, you decide to find out what kind of involvement already takes place there. Therefore, your question is: *How is the local community currently involved in college activity?*

2 You are investigating differentiated teaching in mathematics for high-achieving students within mixed-ability classrooms. Your first research question is: *In these mixed-ability classes, how is work in mathematics differentiated for more able students?*

3 You are researching use of a 'home corner' in a pre-school setting. Your first research question asks: *In what ways does this pre-school setting use the home corner as part of its curriculum?*

 **Key Points**

So this first research question asks: *What is happening already in relation to my topic in the class, school, college or other educational setting where my research will be based?*

Research Question 2: Finding out what your participants think about the different aspects of your topic

Research Question 2 leads on to something different: an examination of the perceptions and opinions of the people involved. For example:

1 You are investigating how students with autism are taught in a special school. You find out about the school's strategies in your first research question. Your second question asks: *In the opinion of staff, what are the advantages and disadvantages of the school's strategies for teaching students with autism?*

2 You are investigating a school's provision of homework. Your second question is: *What are the views about the benefits and difficulties of having homework:*
   a Of students?
   b Of parents?
   c Of teachers?

3 You are investigating how a college uses specialist advisers to enhance their curriculum. Your second question is: *What do advisers feel are the positive and negative aspects of their roles and responsibilities?*

 **Key Points**

So this second research question is asking: *What are the opinions of relevant people about aspects of educational practice relating to my topic?*

'Pluses and minuses': Looking at the whole picture

Notice the paired phrases in these examples: 'advantages and disadvantages'; 'benefits and difficulties'; 'positive and negative aspects'. It is sometimes tempting, especially for educators themselves, to focus only on positive elements of practice, the benefits. However, there are always less positive elements too: disadvantages, obstacles, tensions, even the lack of benefit, the failings. Investigating these lends depth and value to your study. Try, therefore, to look at the whole picture, at the pluses and the minuses. Using a paired phrase in your research questions, as in these examples, is one way of doing this.

Research Question 3: You choose where to go next...

In this suggested framework, you now choose in which direction to take your research. For instance:

1　You are investigating educational support for children in care. For your final research question you ask: *How might educational provision for children in care be further developed?*

2　You are investigating how children from minority cultures are included in a predominantly mono-cultural classroom. You decide to focus your final question on needs for professional development: *How could professional development help educators strengthen their practice in relation to the inclusion of children from minority cultures?*

3　You are investigating the use of podcasting in a college curriculum. For your final research question, you decide to find out in particular: *How can podcasting help students when they revise for examinations?*

 Key Points

So in this third research question, you identify and investigate one specific aspect of your overall topic which will extend or deepen what you have found out from your first and second research questions.

 Ann writes the first draft of her research questions

Ann is investigating ways in which a secondary school communicates with its students' parents and carers. She decides to follow the three-question framework presented above. She uses her first question to find out about the communication strategies already used by the school. Her second question focuses on

(Continued)

(Continued)

the benefits and difficulties of such strategies as perceived by staff and parents or carers. In her third question, she sets out to discover how use of mobile phone technology could improve communication further. Ann's three research questions (in her first draft) are:

1 What strategies are used by the school to communicate with the parents and carers of its students?
2 In the opinions of staff, parents and carers, what are the benefits and difficulties associated with these strategies?
3 How might mobile phone technology be used to strengthen and expand these strategies in the future?

You may notice that in the examples above, one question seems almost to lead to the next. A progressive structure of this kind allows you to research an issue in increasing detail and depth and gives a sense of cohesion to your project as a whole.

Using sub-questions

You will also have noticed that one example above (the question about homework) included sub-questions, marked (a), (b) and (c). In that example, the researcher was using them to identify various groups which would be involved. Another way of using them is to state the exact areas you intend to research, as Sally does here.

 Sally uses sub-questions to define areas for investigation

Sally is investigating outdoor learning in a nursery. Her first research question is: *In what ways does the nursery setting use the outdoor environment to promote children's early development and learning?* She realizes that there are many things she could find out to answer this question, so decides to use sub-questions to identify the particular aspects she will examine. Her improved first research question is:

In what ways does this nursery use the outdoor environment to promote children's early development and learning, in relation to:

> *a The natural environment?*
>
> *b Fixed equipment?*
>
> *c Small toys?*

Other kinds of research questions

The three types of research questions examined so far in this chapter are not the only ones you can use. Here are some other ways in which they can be designed:

Statements: Research questions need not be questions at all – some researchers prefer simple statements or objectives instead. For instance:

- How collaboration with a special school might help a mainstream school to improve its provision for students with disabilities.
- To investigate the opinions of students and staff about college facilities for private study.

Hypotheses: Some research projects state a 'hypothesis', instead of or as well as research questions. A hypothesis is a statement which might be true (or might not). The researcher sets up a 'controlled trial' so that the strength of the statement can be examined. Not surprisingly, this approach is most commonly associated with experimental research and a positivist paradigm (see Chapter 1). Here are some hypotheses which might be examined in this way:

- Students sitting in rows make better progress than when they sit in groups.
- Using practical approaches improves children's learning in mathematics.
- Healthy eating increases children's concentration in afternoon lessons.

Note, however, that research to confirm or disprove a hypothesis is, like the 'cause-and-effect' research we discussed in Chapter 1, normally beyond the scope of beginner researchers and a small-scale project. You could, however, examine participants' perceptions or other evidence about the statement, in the same way as Jeffrey eventually decided to look at 'indications' of a relationship between attendance and achievement in Chapter 4. If you do so, make sure this is clear in how you describe and carry out your project.

Comparisons: If you decide to compare different scenarios, for instance how an element of mathematics is taught in two or more different classes, you can adapt the framework given above in order to design suitable research questions. Your first research question might examine practice in both settings; your second could explore the opinions of staff and children at both settings. Your third could put together or make comparisons between the sets of data and draw overall conclusions about your topic.

Whichever way you choose to phrase your questions, they need to be clear, understandable and accurate, as we discussed earlier. You might want to check the views of your project tutor about how your research questions should be written.

Some further characteristics

As you have worked through this chapter, you may have noticed more important features of research questions. Let us look at these now – there is a short activity for you to undertake in relation to each (suggested answers are in Appendix II):

1. 'Open-ended'

Usually research questions do not imply a simple 'yes' or 'no' response – instead they leave open a wide range of possible answers. For example, examine this research question: *Are strategies used to help students with learning difficulties at this college?* The answer could be 'yes', 'no' or 'I don't know', but not much more. The question would be better phrased like this: *How are strategies to help students with learning difficulties used at this college?* It is now more open-ended and exploratory – a range of answers could be given to this question.

 Activity 5.1   Making research questions open-ended

Here are some 'yes or no' research questions. Rephrase them to make them more open-ended:

1   Are children taught to play a musical instrument at this school?

2   Is training for teaching assistants provided in this nursery?

3   Do students use digital photography in geography lessons?

2. Balanced and objective

Research questions do not betray the researcher's bias. Take this research question, for instance: *Why is synthetic phonics an effective way of teaching children to read?* The question presumes that synthetic phonics is an effective way of teaching children to read. The question might be reasonable if the researcher only wanted to examine evidence that this was the case. In most cases, however, a more objective approach will lead to a more balanced project, for instance: *What are the advantages and disadvantages of using synthetic phonics to help children to learn to read?*

 Activity 5.2   Making research questions balanced and objective

Here are some rather unbalanced or biased research questions. Rephrase them to make them suitable for more impartial investigations:

1 How do formal tests harm the education of young children?

2 Why does use of the college intranet help students to learn?

3 In the views of staff, how does the use of praise ensure that children behave appropriately?

3. Written in correct English

You know this, of course. Indeed, as we will discuss in Chapter 12, the need for correct English applies to your whole written project. However, your research questions are particularly important and deserve very close attention.

 Activity 5.3   Writing research questions correctly

Correct these two research questions (there are two mistakes in each). Answers are in Appendix II.

1 How can the proffessional developement of teachers be improved?

2 In the opinion of teacher's and students, what is the affect of music on behaviour?

Thinking about the project as a whole

There is a final consideration when designing your research questions: that is, to envisage their relationship to your project as a whole. Here are four aspects to this:

1. How to investigate them?

In the previous chapter, I encouraged you to think about possible methods of investigation when choosing your topic. It is worth considering this again when designing your research questions. How could you go about answering them? For example, in relation to Sally's project on outdoor learning above, she might think:

- I can find out about natural features and facilities by examining the outdoor environment and observing children at play.
- I can find out how children's use of this environment is intended to promote development and learning by examining the school's policy documents, by interviewing staff and by looking for evidence in practice.

If you cannot work out how you might investigate your research questions, you should rethink them so they are more answerable through reasonable methods of research (see Chapter 7).

2. Where to investigate them?

It is useful to have a rough idea, even at this early stage, of where you might carry out your investigation. Will you be able to find the information to answer your research questions there? If not, then you may need to rethink them (or rethink your research venue). We examine the process of finding a venue in Chapter 10.

3. When to investigate?

Will you have time to carry out the investigations to answer the questions you have designed? Are any too ambitious, beyond the scope of a small research project, or out of step with your course timetable? Take another look, for instance, at Manisha's problem with timescale in Chapter 4.

4. Are your research questions ethical?

Remember also the importance of not causing harm or disadvantage to your participants or to yourself. If you have any doubts in this respect, then rethink your questions, or discuss the issue with your project tutor.

Project Sheets 4 and 5   Research questions

You should now be ready to complete a first draft of your research questions using Project Sheet 4. Then use Project Sheet 5 to start the process of evaluating these against the checklist of advice about good research questions in this chapter. As you can see, you should revisit this checklist regularly when doing your project. Both of these Project Sheets are in Appendix I.

Development

So there is much to think about in relation to research questions – this simply reflects their importance for your project as a whole. As your work develops, you may find yourself making them more detailed and precise, and more accurate in relation to your project as a whole. Finally, here are examples of research questions which show that kind of refinement. In the main, they follow the framework which we examined above, but you will note some differences too:

Topic 1: Use of a college intranet to promote collaborative learning

1   How does this college use an intranet to promote students' collaborative learning?
2   What are the perceptions of tutors and students about use of this intranet for:
  a   Joint investigation?
  b   Group role-play?
  c   Sharing of reflective journals?
3   How can these collaborative activities be used to assess students' formal progress on their course?

Topic 2: The education of ethnic minority groups in a secondary school

1   What ethnic minority groups can be identified in this year group?
2   How does their school support their learning and achievement in relation to:
  a   Curriculum content?
  b   Parental involvement?
  c   Celebration of cultural events?

3 What evidence is there that these approaches help these students to learn successfully?

Topic 3: Boys' achievement in literacy

1 What are the levels of achievement in literacy of 10- and 11-year-old boys in this school?
2 How do these levels compare with national averages for this type of school?
3 What are the possible reasons for differences between levels of achievement of the school and national averages?
4 What lessons can be learned for further development of practice in this area, at this school or elsewhere?

Looking ahead

Your research questions are the 'backbone' to your study. When you write up your project, you will state them clearly near the start, refer back to them as you progress and eventually present your findings in relation to each of them in turn. We will discuss these and other processes in Chapter 12.

For now, if you have set out a first draft and started using the checklist to check quality, you have made a major step in your research project. You are ready to progress to the next stage: finding out what has been written already about the topic of your research and composing an important part of the written project, your 'literature review'.

Further reading 📖

Andrews, R. (2003) *Research Questions*. London: Continuum.
A short text, but informative and fully focused on the subject of research questions.

Lewis I. and Munn P. (2004) *So You Want to Do Research! Guide for Beginners on How to Formulate Research Questions*. Revised ed. University of Glasgow: The SCRE Centre.
An even shorter text, but equally useful, especially when considering 'Where do research questions come from?'

Thomas, G. (2009) *How to Do Your Research Project*. London: Sage.
Chapter 1 examines in a lively way the design of research questions at the start of your project.

6   Literature review

What will you learn from this chapter?

There are two types of literature which you will find, read and use while doing your project. The first is literature on designing and doing research – you have already seen examples of this in previous chapters. The second relates to the topic of your research. Finding and analysing this literature will strengthen understanding of what you are investigating and be the focus of one particular part of your written project: the 'literature review'.

Literature about your topic

No research stands on its own. Any investigation is just one small part of a much wider and deeper accumulation of knowledge and understanding. Bit by bit, through thousands of research investigations and other texts, we increase, adapt or even completely change our understanding of the world. As Anderson and Arsenault (1998: 76) put it: 'Successful research is based on all the knowledge, thinking and research that precedes it'. Your investigation may be small, but it too is a part of this constant development.

This means that in doing your project, you need to acquire some understanding of what has been written or researched already by others. We call this the 'literature', and it includes any material available to the public in print or online: books; articles in journals, magazines and newspapers; official reports; reports on research (including dissertations and theses); and other Internet material. By analysing literature of this kind, you will appreciate better how your own investigation relates to what has already been written, and help readers of your project to do likewise.

Key Points

Being familiar with published literature and research helps you to see how your investigation relates to work that has already been done or views that have already been expressed, and helps your reader to do the same.

The literature review

The most important part of a research study in this respect is the literature review. It can be found in nearly all research reports. If you did the task in Chapter 3, you will almost certainly have found some kind of literature review in the article you analysed. It is almost certain also that you will be required to do something similar in your own project.

Here are two definitions of a literature review:

'A clear and balanced picture of current leading concepts, theories and data relevant to the topic' (Hart, 1998: 173).

'A critical analysis of existing literature on your proposed research subject ... You find out what has been done (and not done) prior to your research' (Birley and Moreland, 1998: 80).

Here is my definition:

 Key Points

A literature review is a critical analysis of what is understood already about your topic and themes related to it, and of some of the varied perspectives which have been expressed.

Note how a literature review is not a description of the literature, it is a 'critical analysis' of it. We will consider this issue of 'criticality' later in this chapter.

Why have a literature review?

A literature review performs several important functions in your research project. Here are some:

- It clarifies the background or current 'context' of your investigation.
- It enables you to find gaps, misunderstandings or lack of clarity in previous research – perhaps your own study will address some of these limitations.
- It means you are less likely to duplicate other research.
- It allows you to relate the findings of your investigation to what is already known and understood.

We can separate the process of doing your literature review into six stages:

1 Identify relevant literature.
2 Find the literature.
3 Read and analyse it.
4 Structure your literature review.
5 Work on content.
6 Start writing.

We deal with each of these in turn now, with key points, case studies and activities to help you to apply them to your own project.

1. Identify relevant literature

The first step is to work out what kind of literature you need to find and examine. Above, we said that it should 'relate' to the topic you have chosen to investigate. Thinking about what 'relates to' your topic is an important process. One way to do it, as Hollie does in the case study below, is to start with your topic, then work outwards, identifying the wider themes of which it is a part.

Hollie identifies themes which 'relate' to her topic

Hollie is investigating how an education adviser works with classroom teachers to improve the teaching of mathematics in a secondary school. She starts with this topic, then moves in stages to wider related themes, drawing up a list as shown in Figure 6.1.

(Continued)

(Continued)

Advisory work on mathematics with classroom teachers
(the topic of Hollie's project)

⇓

Advisory work with teachers across the curriculum
(widens the focus to look at the broader curriculum role)

⇓

Overall responsibilities of advisers
(widens the focus still further to look at the advisory role as a whole)

⇓

Local, regional, national and international policy on the role of advisory services
(looks at the background to advisers' work at various policy levels)

Figure 6.1 Hollie's themes, relating to her topic

Hollie notes how her themes expand as her list progresses. She knows she must find and read literature about each of the themes in her list in order to understand better the background to her topic and to write her literature review. She knows too that she is researching an area which is subject to change, so her reading must include materials which are up to date.

 Key Points

When you read literature for your project, you read not just about your exact topic, but about its wider context. This is an important process which will help you to structure your literature review.

 Project Sheet 6   Identify relevant literature

Apply the process above to your own project:

1 Start with your chosen topic.

2 Move in stages, identifying wider themes which relate to it.

3 Build a list as Hollie did in the case study, using Project Sheet 6 in Appendix I.

4 End at the bottom of the list with the widest theme of all – the broad context of your research.

2. Find the literature

Now you need to find literature about the themes in your list. There are two main ways of doing this: searching in your library and searching online.

Searching in your library

If you are a student registered at a college or university, it is likely you are already familiar with your library or learning centre. You may have already used its catalogue to search for a particular topic, author, keyword or book title which interests you. This catalogue may only include material which the library has physically in stock, or may also give you access to wider online material through databases to which the library subscribes.

If you are in doubt about how to use the catalogue, or what it includes, then ask your librarian to help. If you are not a registered student, but work in a school, you may still be able to use the local university or college library in this way – contact them and ask if this is possible. Note that many libraries now have electronic copies of well-used books, which you can access online at any time, rather than waiting for a printed copy to become available.

Searching online

In nearly all cases, there is more literature available than is held in your library or accessible through its catalogue. To broaden and deepen your search further, you will need to 'search online'. There are two main aspects to this: searching particular databases to find journal articles relevant to your topic, and searching the Internet as a whole.

A. Searching databases

This kind of search will help you to find relevant material in hundreds of academic journals which publish articles and papers about education.

Why journal articles?

There are several very good reasons why you should be reading and using journal articles:

- Journal articles are more up to date than books – using them will make your project more up to date as well.
- There are more articles than books, so they provide more useful material related to your topic.
- Journal articles attract more critical academic and professional debate. Analysing these debates can add interest and vitality to your project.

Key Points

Using journal articles as part of your reading helps you to include current, critical debate in your literature review which will inform your investigation as a whole.

Databases

Searching online is the best, indeed the only feasible way of finding relevant journal articles. There are many databases (or 'indexes') which you can use, all holding details of published articles in education and many giving access to articles in full. For instance:

- The British Education Index (BEI) is a database of UK publications: www.leeds.ac.uk/bei
- The Education Resources Information Center, commonly known as ERIC, has periodicals from the USA: www.eric.ed.gov
- Educational Research Abstracts online (ERA) covers international research in education: www.tandf.co.uk/journals/titles/14675900.asp

Access

Unfortunately, there is a subscription to access these databases. As an individual, it is unlikely that you will want to pay this. However, all academic libraries subscribe to a range of databases so that their staff and students can use them, usually from on-site computers, and sometimes – with a password – from home as well. If you are unclear about this, ask the library staff to explain what databases are available and how you can access them if they are not part of its catalogue. Again, if you are not a registered student, go to your local university or college and see if they can help.

Doing searches

You have access to online journal databases – here (with the example of Trevor as a guide) is how to search them. If you have already searched for material in your library catalogue, you will find that searching databases directly is a fairly similar process.

1 Think about your topic. What are the main words or terms associated with it? These are known as 'keywords'. Make a list of them.

2 Think about alternatives for these keywords. What other words or terms mean roughly the same? Your computer thesaurus can be helpful here (see Activity 1.1 in Chapter 1). Add these to your list.

3 On your computer, go to a chosen database or databases (your online system may allow you to search several databases at once). Choose to do an 'advanced search', then:

a Enter one of your keywords.

b Choose to search full texts or abstracts or just titles.

c Choose also to search the field of education.

d Choose a date range for articles you wish to find.

e Do a search.

 Trevor's search 1

Trevor is searching for articles on the learning of 'gifted and talented' students, using a database recommended by his library but not part of its electronic catalogue. He chooses first to do a basic search and enters his keyword: 'gifted'. He limits the search to the abstracts of articles about education published since 2007.

To continue...

4 If you are lucky, a manageable number of journal articles (called 'hits') will come up. You can view details of those which interest you and sometimes see the article as a whole.

5 If you are not lucky, you will either have very few articles (or even no hits at all), or a very long list – too many to look through efficiently.

6 **If you have too few**, there are various things you can do:

• Enter a different word from your list and see what you find.

• Combine keywords using the OR facility – this means that you can search for articles which have either of the words you enter.

• Extend the dates you have specified, or extend the scope of the search to full texts.

7 **If your search has produced too many hits**, you need to limit your next search. Again, you can do this in several ways:

• Use the AND facility. This searches for publications which have both or all your specified words – there will therefore be fewer of such articles.

- Use the NOT facility – this means you can search for articles which have one of the words but not the other.
- If you searched in full texts, limit your next search to abstracts or titles, or narrow down the date of publications.

8 You can search in other ways too:

- **Title search:** If you already know the title of an article, enter this, or part of it, in the 'Title' box.
- **Author search:** If you wish to find articles by a particular author, enter her or his last name in the 'Author' box and do a search. All articles on this database by this author (and of course other authors with the same name) will be listed.
- **Combinations:** You can combine title, author and keywords, entering search words in each, to narrow down your search even further.
- **'Truncation':** Entering one part of a keyword (sometimes followed by a symbol) can bring up all forms of that word. If searching on the British Education Index, for example, 'educ*' brings up education, educational, educating, and so on.

 Trevor's search 2

Trevor's first keyword search for 'gifted' produced 110 hits – rather too many to look through properly. He decides to narrow his search by combining keywords from his list. He specifies that the articles must include both 'gifted' AND 'learning' – 26 hits; 'gifted' AND 'talented' – 19 hits. Now Trevor is getting reasonable numbers and can identify those most relevant to his study.

Whatever searches you do, it is worthwhile keeping a record of them. This means that you can repeat particular searches at another time, or avoid replicating them. The database may itself keep a record to save or print off. It may also offer a facility for alerting you by email when new articles, relevant to your interests, become available.

 Trevor decides which journal articles to use

Trevor identifies five journal articles closely related to his research topic. He decides that two are not worth examining:

one was published in 1995 and is no longer very relevant; the other seems rather superficial. The other three are much more promising. The first of these discusses important aspects of his topic from a variety of perspectives and reaches some well-balanced judgements. The second is written by a well-known educator who has written other material on this theme. The third was published in 2001 but will help Trevor to include a historical perspective to his discussion.

B. Searching the Internet as a whole

You can also use wider aspects of the Internet to find further information and literature relating to your project. For instance:

- **Google Scholar** (click on 'more' on the main Google page – Scholar is in the drop-down menu) helps you search for material on a chosen subject and may tell you where it can be obtained.
- **Gateways** and **portals** offer information and links to material about particular themes. See, for instance, those listed by the Institute of Education, London, at www.ioe.ac.uk/services/570.html
- **Catalogues** of many libraries are available across the Internet, for instance Oxford University: http://library.ox.ac.uk. See also the Integrated Catalogue of the British Library: http://blpc.bl.uk. To get material from libraries like these, use the system of 'inter-library loan' – ask at your library about this (there may be a small charge).
- **Summaries of published research** are often held online, such as the NFER and CERUKplus archives referred to in Chapter 1.
- **Theses and dissertations**: http://www.theses.com
- **Conference papers**: for instance, those held by The Open University at http://library.open.ac.uk/find/confepapers
- **Journal listings**: do an Internet search for 'journals education'. Commercial publishers have their own listings, for instance: http://www.tandf.co.uk/journals
- **Alerting or current awareness services**: many institutions and publishers will send you regular emails showing the latest articles relating to your interests, for instance the Zetoc Alerts of the British Library: http://zetoc.mimas.ac.uk and JournalTOCs: www.journaltocs.hw.ac.uk
- **Official publications** are available, for instance: www.official-documents.gov.uk
- **Newspapers** are held online, for instance the *Times Educational Supplement*: www.tes.co.uk. Your library may subscribe to these and

others are freely available. They can help you examine the importance or topicality of particular issues.

- **Professional networks:** educationalists increasingly use micro-blogs such as Twitter and Tumblr, the Academia network (www.academia. edu), and business-related social networks such as LinkedIn to share materials and ideas.

Suitability

Trevor did not just find literature but also evaluated its suitability for his project. You should do the same. Here are some questions to ask yourself:

- **Is it relevant?** What is the material about exactly? For instance, if you are investigating educational policy in England, make sure the material is not about policy in another country: Scotland or the USA, for example.
- **Is it up to date?** Generally, you should be looking at material published in the last few years. Sometimes, as in Hollie's example above, you will want this to include very recent material, even education newspapers or magazines, in order to keep up with current change and development. Occasionally too, you will want older material – publications, for instance, which remain very relevant to education today, or which may help you to trace historical development of your topic in your literature review. Remember that many well-read books are published in several editions – you will normally want to consult the most recent of these.
- **Is it dependable?** Another judgement to make relates to the trustworthiness of the material you examine. It should appear thoughtful, accurate and generally well-balanced; views expressed should be based on reasonable assumptions or evidence and argued in a rational way (even if you do not agree with them). In most cases, authors should quote other sources and give references for those sources. If the material is on the Internet, a URL which includes '.ac', '.edu', '.gov' or '.org' is more likely to have appropriate and usable material of this kind than other sites.
- **Who has written it?** Is the authorship clear? Is she or he (or they) experienced and respected in their field? What are the motives in writing this material – are these reasonable, or is the author pursuing a strong political or social agenda which excludes other perspectives? Note that 'wiki' websites, such as Wikipedia, are written anonymously by users. While the material can be interesting and useful in some contexts, this means we cannot trust it fully – it may be unduly biased or simply incorrect. Do not reference 'wiki' or similar websites in your project – they are not dependable enough to use as a basis for academic writing.

There may nevertheless be some occasions when you do want to look at less trustworthy literature. For instance:

- You may wish to examine views expressed in polemical literature (polemical literature contains strongly worded and passionate argument against or in favour of an issue), perhaps to illustrate the more extreme views which are held about your topic.
- You may wish to examine more informal literature from the media, for instance a tabloid newspaper, perhaps to illustrate how a particular theme is reported in popular culture.

Understanding your sources

Even when you have chosen suitable literature to examine, there is another aspect to consider: the intentions of whoever is writing or publishing it. For instance:

- Government publications (found on those '.gov' websites) will usually reflect official perspectives and even try to portray current government policy in a positive light (see Scott, 2000, for an interesting discussion of how this is often done). To balance this, you may also wish to consult other literature which takes a more objective or critical stance on the issues discussed.
- Research sponsored by a business or other organization may be designed to support their particular views. Again, you may wish to search more widely to get a better balance.

 Key Points

You should assess carefully whether literature is useful and appropriate for your project. In most cases, the material you examine should be thoughtful, balanced, well researched and written by an author or authors respected in their field. It is also worthwhile considering the intentions behind the publication and taking these into account when examining it.

---

3. Read and analyse it

You have worked out your themes and found relevant and dependable literature. Now you read it, and, even more importantly, you 'analyse' it. Hart (1998: 110) calls analysis 'the job of systematically breaking down something into its constituent parts and describing how they relate to each other'.

Imagine dismantling an engine and then laying out the pieces: all those to do with steering together, all the electronic parts together, and so on. You will not have an engine, but you will understand better the various components which make it work. In the same way, 'taking text apart' will help you to understand and assess what writers say and how their views ('perspectives') coincide or differ. You gain 'critical understanding' of ideas related to your topic which you can pass on to your reader.

 **Key Points**

> When doing research, you should analyse the literature you have identified. Analysis involves breaking down the text to see what ideas are expressed, and making connections or comparisons to see how perspectives coincide or diverge. These are essential steps in preparing your literature review.

Breaking down

To analyse text, you need – in one way or another – to read and take notes. This is the 'breaking down' part of analysis. Here is a staged approach to this process:

1 First make a note of what you are reading (as you did if you completed the task in Chapter 3):
   - For a **book**: author's name, year of publication, book title, place of publication, name of publisher.
   - For a **chapter in an edited book**: the author of the chapter and the chapter's title, as well as details of the book itself.
   - For a **journal article**: author's name, year of publication, title of article, title of journal, volume number, issue number, page numbers of article.
   - For **Internet material**: author's name (or owner of website), date (if you can find one), title of material, URL address, date when you downloaded it.

You will need all this information when you reference your material in your written project – we cover this in detail in Chapter 12.

2 Determine exactly what you want to read about. It is not a good use of time if you plough through a 300-page book when you are only interested in one particular aspect. Scan the introduction, and use chapter headings and the index to find the parts you wish to examine.

3 Decide how you will take notes from your reading:

- on your computer (this is my preferred way as I can then easily manipulate my notes into real text)
- by hand in a notebook
- (if the material belongs to you) by scribbling in the text and margin.

4 Decide on your strategies for taking notes. For example:

- Pick out, highlight or underline the main issues being discussed.
- Note what the author says about these – their 'perspective' or 'argument'.
- Copy or highlight any useful phrase which you might use as a quote (note the page number too – you will need it if you use the phrase as a quotation in your written project).
- Add your own thoughts. For instance, you may identify a possible weakness in the author's argument, or a particular strength in the evidence presented, or you may identify a specific idea which you wish to examine further elsewhere.

Making connections

When you have notes on several publications, you are ready to start thinking about the literature review itself. Your project is, for instance, about the use of technology in education. You have examined relevant literature and found discussion about these four issues: hardware, software, benefits and practical obstacles. You now need to re-organize your notes according to these themes – this is the 'making connections' part of analysis.

Again, you can do this on paper or on your computer. In this example, list the four themes: 'Hardware'; 'Software'; 'Benefits'; 'Practical obstacles'. Now under 'Hardware', make a note of everything which each publication says about this theme. Now do the same with 'Software', again with 'Benefits' and again with 'Practical obstacles'.

With a computer, you can cut and paste your notes to reorganize them in this way (but always keep a record of the publication from which each idea is taken). With written notes, you can code your notes using different coloured pens, or with numbers: 'Hardware' = 1; 'Software' = 2; 'Benefits' = 3; 'Practical obstacles' = 4. All the parts marked 1 will relate to 'Hardware', whilst all those marked 2 will relate to 'Software', and so on.

You can then work out how different perspectives about a single theme relate to each other. Do authors agree or say the same thing (agreement) or do they disagree or take a different view (contrast)? Or while agreeing, do they have different kinds of emphasis, or just look at the same issue from different angles, for instance from the perspective of parents, rather than professionals, or from children rather than adults?

Key Points

Grouping your notes according to main themes, rather than according to each author, will help you to focus on ideas. You will be able to identify how different writers view the same themes: do they agree, disagree, vary in emphasis, or look at things in different ways? These are important considerations for your literature review.

 Activity 6.1 Vygotsky's ideas

Below are some brief notes about the ideas of the psychologist, Lev Vygotsky, drawn from some imaginary authors. Working on your own or with a colleague, find areas of agreement or contrast between these ideas. Then have a go at turning them into continuous text about Vygotsky's theories on the role of teachers and others in children's learning. A sample answer is given in Appendix II.

One of Vygotsky's main contributions to our understanding of learning is the concept of the 'zone of proximal development' (Brown, 2003).

In most cases what Vygotsky terms 'knowledgeable others' means the teacher (Green, 2008).

Vygotsky's zone of proximal development refers to the gap between what an individual can do alone and what can be achieved with 'knowledgeable others' (White, 2006: 27).

The research study by Black (2009) concludes that a range of adults play an important role in children's learning.

'When considering the important role of the teacher in Vygotsky's ideas, we must be careful not to devalue the contribution of others, such as assistants, parents, even peers' (Gold, 2010: 65).

'It is dialogue which is important, the children must be able to exchange thoughts and ideas with others' (Amber, 2012: 34).

Observation of 50 secondary-school classes by Lavender (2010) highlighted the teacher's crucially important role in helping children to learn.

4. Structure your literature review

You have taken notes, organized them according to themes and found connections. Now it is time to turn these reorganized notes into a literature review. If you did the Vygotsky activity above, you have already practised the techniques involved. Here are some features of this very important part of your project:

- A literature review is like a short essay on themes related to your chosen research topic.
- It is carefully structured and coherent.
- It is largely organized according to ideas: you discuss what a range of authors says about one idea, then move on to discussing what authors say about another idea.
- It shows areas of agreement and contrast, including variations in emphasis and perspective.
- It focuses on the literature – you do not discuss your own experiences and opinions.
- Nevertheless, it does include judgements of your own – we will discuss this later in the chapter.

Structure

The structure of your literature review is important. If it is logically organized, the reader will enjoy reading it. If it is disjointed or confused, the reader will have considerable difficulty understanding what you write. To make your structure clear and logical:

- Divide the literature review into sections and give each section a short and concise heading.
- List these headings before you start to write. As you write, add text under the appropriate heading.

'The Funnel'

There is a third important process: deciding the order in which to set out your review. There is no 'right' way to do this, but if you are unsure, you may like to work through my recommendation, which I call 'The Funnel'.

A funnel has a wide top and a narrow bottom. This can be a good way of thinking about your literature review: at the start you deal with the big, wide issues related to your topic, then you gradually focus in until you come to the narrow, closely defined topic of your own investigation. This may remind you of what I wrote earlier when advising you on your reading. Then I suggested that you start with your topic, then think progressively about the wider issues which relate to it. Indeed, the structure for your written literature review is the same – it is just that now we turn it the other way round. Start broad and focus in.

Hollie finds a structure for her literature review

We met Hollie and her mathematics-adviser investigation at the start of this chapter. She drew up a list of themes to read about, which started with her topic and expanded in scope. Now she is planning the structure of her literature review. For this, she simply turns the list she made for her reading upside down: see Figure 6.2.

Local, regional, national and international policy on the role of advisory services
(the widest issue)

⇓

Overall responsibilities of advisers
(focuses in on the role of advisers in general)

⇓

Advisory work with teachers across the curriculum
(focuses in further on the role of advisers with teachers)

⇓

Advisory work on mathematics with classroom teachers
(the topic of Hollie's research)

Figure 6.2   Hollie's structure for her literature review

Hollie now has a 'funnel' of ideas which provides a structure for her literature review. She will review the literature about each theme in this order.

Project Sheet 7   A structure for your literature review

Project Sheet 7 in Appendix I helps you to design a structure for your literature review, with Hollie's example as a guide. Complete the third column with your own themes – these may be similar or even the same as the ones you listed earlier in Project Sheet 6, just in the opposite order. Add further rows if you wish to have additional steps.

5. Work on content

What should you include in each section? Here is guidance, related to what we have discussed so far:

- In each paragraph, write about a particular idea.
- Say what one author says about this idea.
- Say what another says about it.
- Indicate how these perspectives relate to each other, for example the extent and nature of agreement or contrast between them, or differences in emphasis or perspective.
- Use link words to lead your reader through this discussion, for example: 'similarly', 'in addition' (to indicate agreement); 'however', 'on the other hand' (to indicate contrast).

Exploring key concepts

One particular aspect of content deserves special mention: exploring key concepts. This is because a single word or concept can mean different things to different people. Take the word 'vehicle', for instance. That includes cars and lorries, of course. Does it include trains? Bicycles? Roller skates? Opinions may differ, so when you say 'vehicle', people may envisage this concept in different ways.

Similarly in research, perceptions can differ, and it can be useful to explore these differences in the literature review. For instance, you can critically examine the outlooks of other writers, or gather together features of the concept to build up a picture of what it involves (I did something similar when discussing the meaning of 'research' in Chapter 1).

 Carol builds understanding of the concept of 'inclusion'

Carol's research project is about 'inclusion', the notion that an educational setting can and should meet the needs of the whole of its community, including students with disabilities or who are disadvantaged in some way. She notes that in the literature there are different perceptions about what 'inclusion' involves. She decides to take notes on these perspectives, then

(Continued)

(Continued)

reorganize her notes to find agreement and contrast in the way described in this chapter. This is what she finds:

- Author A suggests that inclusion involves different students 'learning successfully together' (Carol underlines this concise and useful quote, and notes the page number).
- Author B says that it involves all students participating alongside each other in classroom activity.
- Author C says that inclusion is about students with disabilities having the right to be educated alongside non-disabled peers.

Carol notes that the three perspectives on inclusion have similarities and differences. One similarity is that they all emphasize a notion of 'togetherness': Author A uses the word 'together', whilst Authors B and C prefer 'alongside'. The authors differ, however, in their view of its rationale: Author A emphasizes successful learning; Author B emphasizes participation; Author C emphasizes students' human rights, in particular the rights of those with disabilities. Carol feels that the first standpoint could be termed 'pedagogical', the second 'social', the last 'civil' or 'political'. All three help Carol to build up an understanding of this important concept in relation to education, and she is able to share this increased understanding with readers through her literature review.

 Key Points

Analyse the literature closely to see how key concepts are perceived. Showing how commentators understand the same concept in different ways can be a valuable outcome of your literature review.

Making judgements: 'criticality'

We said earlier that your own opinions do not usually form part of the literature review. This is not quite true. You can and should include judgements of your own, not about the ideas you are discussing, but about the literature you are analysing. For instance (using imaginary references):

- If an argument is convincing, you might write: 'Smith (2012) has stated persuasively that…'
- If an argument appears rather biased, you might write: 'Smith (2012) over-emphasizes the views of…'
- If an argument is energetically stated, you might write: 'Smith (2012) has claimed vigorously that…'

This is a part of the important notion of 'criticality' and its associated phrase 'critical analysis'. Criticality has many meanings in different disciplines – here is my definition in relation to research:

 Key Points

> Criticality is the process of evaluating the quality, value and implications of ideas and how they are expressed. It helps you to contribute in constructive ways to debate about them.

You may feel that there is a tension here with the notions of balance and objectivity which we discussed in Chapter 5. We often think of the researcher as standing back and not letting personal values and opinions get in the way of neutral investigation. Indeed, when we come to your research methodology in later chapters, this will again be an important consideration.

However, objectivity is not the only factor in research – and some researchers would claim that it is not fully possible anyway. For instance, in your literature review *you* choose which literature to examine and which to ignore. When you consider those ideas in that literature, *you* work out what they mean and what they imply. When you analyse the data you collect, *you* decide how to interpret such data (as we will see in Chapter 11). If you think about it, none of this is a recipe for 'objective' research.

Now, as you evaluate what authors write about your topic, you might feel you are again straying from a proper objective position. In a way you are, but this can be a positive feature in your study. It is an indication of how researchers make careful judgements and convey these to their readers. It is 'yourself' as the researcher coming through in your study. As Dunne, Pryor and Yates (2005: 15) have written: 'We are not dealing with a fixed and exterior social world, but a world of meaning where the actors are constantly in the process of social construction; and where the researcher is ineluctably [unavoidably] one of those actors'.

Importantly, however, this criticality is always carefully, often 'minimally', expressed. Single words or short phrases, as in the examples above, are often sufficient to make such judgements. Do not use the words 'I' or 'my' in this section, and do not include accounts of your own experience or direct expressions of your own opinions on the themes being covered. Your criticality in this section should be directed towards the literature itself.

Activity 6.2   Trevor's literature review

Trevor's project was about 'gifted and talented' children in England. Below is a first draft of the beginning of his literature review, where he looks at past and present definitions of this term. Look at it carefully and try to find the following aspects of analysis and criticality in his text (my suggested answer is in Appendix II):

1 A useful historical perspective

2 An interesting contrast

3 A useful agreement

4 A well argued judgement

5 A relevant definition which Trevor may be able to use as the basis for his project as a whole.

Early definitions of very able children, for example Rowlands (1974), stressed a child's current ability. However, Montgomery (1996) sought a definition which included what a child might achieve but did not yet demonstrate. Similarly, Freeman (2001) said we should think of children in terms of their future rather than their present performance. This outlook has made it possible to stress the importance of providing challenging educational activities so that ability can emerge: students 'will rarely manifest high ability unless they have the opportunity to do so' (Fletcher-Campbell, 2003: 3). A recent official definition in England reflected this dual outlook: gifted and talented children are those 'with one or more abilities developed to a level significantly ahead of their year group (or with the potential to develop those abilities)' (Department for Children, Schools and Families, 2008: 6).

6. Start writing!

You are now ready to write some draft text for your own literature review, using your completed Project Sheet 7 as a structure. Some last advice (for now) to help with this:

- **Read other literature reviews:** One of the best ways to see how a literature review can be written is to read those written by others. Use the search procedures outlined in this chapter to find suitable examples – study carefully how they are structured and composed.

- **Use sub-titles:** As suggested at the start of this chapter, these help you to organize your text. You can keep or delete them in your final version.

- **Be exact:** When describing a piece of published research, include specific (but concise) detail about the investigation. For instance: 'From a survey of 100 students aged 14–16, Jones (2010) concluded that…'.

- **Always reference:** Whenever you write about someone else's ideas, you must provide a reference to show where those ideas have come from. If you do not, you risk being accused of plagiarism: passing off someone else's thinking or writing as your own. We deal with this important issue more fully in Chapter 12.

Finally, a short reminder of this chapter's main points:

Key Points

In your literature review, write about ideas expressed in a range of literature, structured around a series of themes related to your topic, and integrate judgements on the quality of the arguments into your text.

Start writing!

Further reading 📖

Hart, C. (2001) *Doing a Literature Search: A Comprehensive Guide for the Social Sciences.* London: Sage.
I have cited Hart's book *Doing a Literature Review* (Hart, 1998) in this chapter. This later book is another very useful guide from the same author, covering manual and computerized methods of searching the literature, even though some of the detail is gradually being overtaken by technological change. It is suitable for the beginner as well as the advanced researcher.

Jesson, J.K., Matheson, L. and Lacey, F.M. (2011) *Doing your Literature Review: Traditional and Systematic Techniques.* London: Sage.
This book guides readers through the production of either a literature review within a project, or a self-standing systematic review of research of the kind I described in Chapter 1.

Judge, B., Jones, P. and McCreery, E. (2009) *Critical Thinking Skills for Education Students*. Exeter: Learning Matters.
This short, accessible text outlines how you can develop 'criticality' in your thinking and writing. There is also a section on critical analysis of data, which will help you when we discuss these processes in Chapter 11.

Silverman, D. (2010) *Doing Qualitative Research*. 3rd ed. London: Sage.
David Silverman is a leading writer on research. Chapter 18 deals with the literature review and demonstrates his often distinctive advice.

7 Choosing your methods

What will you learn from this chapter?

To carry out research, you need to choose methods for doing so. In this chapter, we examine some you should consider, such as question-naires, interviews and observations, and the advantages and disadvantages of each. We also look at 'sampling' – deciding who you would like to take part in your investigation.

Methods and data

Let us first clarify a few basic terms:

- **Methodology** is the range of methods and procedures you use to investigate your topic and find answers to your research questions.
- **Data** are the information which you get from these methods.
- **Data collection** is the process of collecting this information.
- **Participants** or **respondents** are the people who take part in these methods and provide your data.

There are many different methods of collecting data in research, and new ways are constantly being discussed and tried out. The main ones which you will be considering for your project are questionnaires, inter-views, observation, document analysis and testing. Methods such as these produce two kinds of data:

- **Quantitative:** This kind is usually numerical, for instance: How many respondents disagreed with the statement: *Mathematics is the most important subject in the curriculum*? Answer: 15.

- **Qualitative:** These data consist of words (or visual images), for instance:
  - ○ A respondent wrote: 'I find teaching mixed-ability classes very difficult'.
  - ○ A participant said: 'The lesson went largely to plan'.
  - ○ Your record of an observation: 'Teacher praised child for correct answer' (but if you were counting the number of times this happened, you would then have quantitative data).

Relating this back to Chapter 1, quantitative data are usually associated with a positivist paradigm; qualitative data with an interpretivist paradigm. Quantitative data can be collected from many respondents; qualitative data usually come from fewer people but allow more in-depth consideration of ideas. We now examine the main methods of collecting both kinds and the pros and cons of each of these methods.

1. Questionnaires

Questionnaires are sets of written questions designed by the researcher which participants answer in writing. This might involve choosing from a selection of responses (for instance, ticking a box), or writing sentences about information and opinions, or a mixture of both. There are several ways of administering questionnaires, for instance:

- **Face-to-face:** You give your respondents a printed questionnaire and wait while they fill it in, or someone else does this for you in your absence.
- **By post or email:** You send out the questionnaire, for instance for parents to complete at home.
- **Online:** You make your questionnaire available online. Software for this is increasingly available, free or at a cost (search online for 'online survey software').

Advantages

Questionnaires can be very useful – that is why we see so many of them in our everyday lives. For instance:

- People understand the process and most (children in particular) are willing to complete them if the procedure is clear and straightforward.
- You can use them to get both kinds of data, qualitative and quantitative.
- You can (and should) use them with a large number of respondents – this is usually known as a questionnaire 'survey'.
- In most cases, everyone answers the same questions. You can therefore quite easily make comparisons between the responses you get.

- Once designed, you can use them as many times as you wish.
- The data you gather can inform more in-depth investigation using other methods.

Disadvantages

Questionnaires look easy to design and to use, but are not. As Hart (1998: 6) wrote: 'You cannot simply write a questionnaire as if you are writing a shopping list'. For instance:

- They take time, effort and skill to design well – you need to be prepared for this.
- They are inflexible – once designed and given out, they cannot be changed.
- There are limits to what people can or wish to write – the qualitative data you get from them can therefore be limited and superficial.
- In some situations, 'response rate' (the number of people who actually complete your questionnaire) can be low.
- The answers given are easily influenced by respondents' mood, the questionnaire design and other factors.

 Activity 7.1   Examining a questionnaire

Next time you receive a market-research questionnaire, examine it closely:

- How are the questions designed?
- Which questions ask for quantitative data? Which ask for qualitative data?
- Fill in the questionnaire: How easy was it to do? How long did it take?
- How long do you think it took to design the questionnaire? How might the designer have tested its suitability for general use?

 Key Points

Questionnaires look easy but are not. You need to spend time and effort designing and testing them to make sure they will give you useful data. Use them only if you are ready for this.

2. Interviews

Interviews are conversations between the researcher and interviewees, usually with the researcher asking questions which the interviewees answer or discuss. There are various types of interviews:

- **structured interviews**, where the researcher prepares all questions in advance and the interviewee answers them one by one
- **unstructured interviews**, where researcher and interviewee explore broad areas related to the research topic, without prior planning of questions
- **semi-structured interviews**, which are somewhere in between. The researcher prepares the main questions beforehand, but during the interview may ask additional questions, or discuss additional topics, not specifically planned in advance.

If you decide to use interviews in your project, your most likely option is the semi-structured kind. These allow you to plan some set questions, but also to pursue new lines of enquiry in response to what your interviewees say. Whatever their structure, interviews do not have to be one-to-one, face-to-face conversations – here are some other ways of carrying them out:

- **Group**: The researcher asks questions to two or more people at the same time (for beginner researchers this is usually the best approach when interviewing children).
- **Focus group**: A pre-determined group of people who debate amongst themselves the issues raised by the researcher.
- **Electronically**: This can be by email, instant messaging, video-conferencing or telephone.

Interviews may also not be just about talking. The researcher can use objects, documents or other materials to prompt and stimulate discussion. For instance, you could:

- discuss a document, such as a school or college policy: *What do you see as the strong and weak points of policy on this issue?*
- examine or discuss examples of students' work: *In this piece of writing, what do you feel are the areas in need of improvement?*
- set a small task: *Please sort these words into their order of importance in relation to your work* – then discuss how the interviewee completed it.

Advantages

Interviews are useful ways of collecting mainly qualitative data. For instance:

- They allow you to explore interviewees' attitudes, opinions and feelings.
- They allow you to discuss these in depth, especially if you are prepared to interrogate closely.
- Unless you are using structured interviews, you do not have to ask the same questions to everyone. You can adapt them from one interview to the next or even while one is taking place, pursuing the information which is most useful for your research and which you feel the interviewee can provide.

Disadvantages

However:

- When interviewing, you can easily be drawn into agreement with your interviewee and lose your neutral stance.
- Recording your data can be problematic – taking notes and voice recording can both be difficult (see Chapter 8).
- People often enjoy talking – it can sometimes be hard to keep the interview on track.
- You can end up with a large amount of textual data. How do you then separate out what is important and useful and what is not?

 Activity 7.2   Trudi's interviews

Trudi wants to interview three sets of people: the headteacher, a specialist music teacher and a group of children, in order to explore how music is taught at her school. Consider what type of interviews might be best to use. Would all the interviews be the same? How might they differ?

 Key Points

Interviews can be a useful way of exploring people's experiences, perspectives and opinions in depth. Designing them well includes deciding how to carry them out and what questions to ask.

3. Observation

Observation 'involves the researcher watching, recording and analysing events of interest' (Blaxter et al., 2010: 199). In educational research, this can be done in classrooms, meeting rooms, the playground or other environments. As with interviews, there are different kinds:

- **Structured**: You know in advance exactly what you are looking out for. For example, while observing a lesson you note down every occasion when a particular student answers a question. Or you actually set up a situation or task, and observe only how participants respond to it.
- **Unstructured**: You observe and record everything that is happening for later analysis.
- **Semi-structured**: As with questionnaires, semi-structured lies somewhere between structured and unstructured. You have a particular area of interest and note down events you observe relating to this. However, you may also record other aspects which seem interesting or relevant.
- **Non-participant**: You watch what is going on without getting involved.
- **Participant**: You take part in the event, such as a meeting, which you are observing.

Advantages

Observation gives you data about '"real life" in the real world', according to C. Robson (2011: 316). Also:

- Like interviewing, it is a flexible approach – you can change your focus if it helps your research.
- It can give you a variety of data, qualitative or quantitative.
- You can observe not just what people do but also what they say and how they interact: if the teacher does this, what do the students do?
- The data you gather can confirm, extend or contradict other data. For instance, observation helps you to see in real life what participants have mentioned in interviews or questionnaires.

Disadvantages

However:

- Some see the approach as intrusive and may not wish to be observed.
- It can be difficult to observe objectively – you may see what you wish to see and ignore what does not fit your prior ideas.

- Social behaviour is complex (and classroom activity particularly so). It can be difficult to make sense of it all. Furthermore, your actual presence may influence what takes place: 'How do we know what the behaviour would have been like if it hadn't been observed?' (C. Robson, 2011: 317).

Activity 7.3   Ben's observations

Ben is investigating how the activity of male and female students differs in science lessons. What kind of observation could he carry out? What aspects of behaviour might he look out for?

Key Points

Observations help researchers investigate real-life situations. Educational activity is complicated, so it is important that you have worked out beforehand what exactly you wish to observe.

4. Document analysis

Analysing documents involves examining what people have written or created and using the results of your analysis as data. Educational documents which you might scrutinize in this way include:

- prospectuses, policy documents or inspection reports
- timetables, lesson plans
- minutes from meetings, letters, emails
- students' writing, drawing or other work
- government documentation, for example curriculum guidance
- websites, newspapers, journal articles
- photographs, displays and other illustrative material
- data collected and published for other research, including published statistics and census records (for instance, UK information available at www.statistics.gov.uk and www.census.ac.uk). These would be called 'secondary data' as they are not your own; the data you collect for your own investigation is called 'primary data'.

Advantages

- Document analysis can give you factual information, for instance the number of students attending a college, or, if you examine older documents, provide a historical perspective.
- It allows you to make use of data which already exist, for instance students' examination results.
- It can tell you about cultural values and practices (see Mary's case study below).
- You can compare data from documents with data from other sources. For instance, to what extent does written policy relate to what is observed in practice?

Disadvantages

However:

- Access to relevant documentation may be restricted because of confidentiality or copyright.
- Data from documents are 'second-hand' and may not reflect actual situations.
- You do not always know why the writer of the document wrote as they did. For instance, is a government document written objectively, or to support official policy?
- Data from other research may not be usable – you are relying on others having done their investigations well.

 Mary uses document analysis as her main method of data collection

Mary is not using human participants in her research. Instead, she is basing her project on analysis of newspapers. She wishes to explore perceptions of the popular national press about the education of teenage boys over the last 12 months. She uses the Internet and her city library to find newspapers which meet her definition of 'popular press' and trawls through them for relevant articles and features. Her analysis will identify and discuss some major characteristics of media perceptions of this theme. Mary will be interested in consulting McCulloch's (2004) guide to the use of written documentation (including newspapers) in educational research.

5. Testing

A test is a set of questions or problems used to assess the abilities or performance of an individual or group. The researcher may, for instance:

- design a test or task for participants to complete
- ask participants to complete a published test, for example government educational tests used in previous years
- evaluate students' work completed during normal classroom activity
- ask participants to complete two (or more) tests over a period of time, so that gains in knowledge, understanding or skills can be determined.

Advantages

- Tests can help you find out what people know, understand and can do, and the extent to which their expertise may have grown over a period of time.
- They allow comparisons to be made between the understanding of different groups, for example male and female students.
- The results can contribute to evaluation of the impact of particular educational approaches (but are unlikely to 'prove' such impact on their own).

Disadvantages

However:

- Participants may feel threatened by being tested, especially if the process appears to cast doubt on their professional or personal abilities.
- Designing your own test needs to be carefully done so that it allows you to assess precisely participants' understanding.
- If you wish to use a published test, you may need special training to do so.
- Testing may encourage 'cause-and-effect' research, which I warned about in Chapter 1. Remember that you need controlled environments to examine the extent to which a particular way of working has 'caused' any improvement which might be evident in test results.

6. Other methods

If you are reading widely, or did the optional task in Chapter 3, you may have come across other methods which you might consider for your project, either as separate approaches or combined with others. Here are some examples:

- **Diary**: Keep a diary, or ask your participants to do so. For example, in a project to evaluate a teaching approach, you ask teachers to write or talk about their experiences and impressions at the end of each lesson.
- **Narratives**: You compose, share and discuss stories, notes, letters, photographs and other materials with participants, in order to find out more about their experiences and views of the world. Narratives are often associated with ethnographic research (see Chapter 1).
- **'Graffiti walls'**: One student I tutored fixed large sheets of paper on the wall and encouraged participants to write comments or answers to questions on them. Children in particular responded enthusiastically to this approach. Something similar could also be done online.
- **'Mosaic'**: Participants share information to show what life is like for them. This is done in several ways, for instance through observation, conversation, objects, drawings, and participants themselves taking photographs and film. Clark and Moss (2005) used this multi-method approach to explore young children's understandings of their outdoor environment.

Choosing your methods

With an understanding of what methods are available, you are now ready to start choosing which to use in your investigation. Here are some more factors to consider when making these important decisions.

Will your methods help you to answer your research questions?

This is a key consideration. If a method will help you to answer your research questions, it is worth considering. If it will not, it is not. For instance:

- If one of your research questions is about current practice, you may choose to use observation to find out what people do, and interviews to explore their perceptions of what they do.
- If one research question is about students' progress, you may choose to examine achievement data collected elsewhere (document analysis) or give students a short test of your own.
- If one question is about professional training, you may choose to use a questionnaire or interviews to ask staff to identify or discuss their needs in this area.

 **Key Points**

> When choosing a research method, ask yourself: Will this method help me answer one or more of my research questions? The answer must be yes, if you are to use that method.

Are your chosen methods ethical?

This is another important question, of course. Whatever methods you choose, they should not bring harm, embarrassment or disadvantage to your participants or indeed to yourself. For instance, asking children questions about the stress of taking national tests may itself increase their worry and concern. A different strategy, perhaps observing their teacher discussing this issue as part of normal classroom activity, might be a more ethical approach.

Are your methods practical?

You need to be as sure as you can be that you will have access to a suitable educational environment and to people for these methods; also that you will have time to carry them out.

How will you analyse data from your chosen methods?

Whatever research methods you choose, give some thought now to how you will use the data from your methods, once collected. You may need to look through Chapter 11 to consider this issue.

Are your choices informed by literature on doing research?

Throughout this book, I have encouraged you to use the literature on doing research to inform your project planning. You should use this literature in particular when considering your research methodology, firstly so you can make the right choices, and secondly – importantly – so you can justify them. The reader of your project will want to know not just what you decided to do, but why you decided to do it. Why questionnaires rather than interviews? Why interviewing and observing children, but not testing their knowledge and understanding? Note that unlike most of the literature on your topic (see Chapter 6), some of the literature on doing research which you consult could have been published several years ago – this is because literature on doing research can remain relevant and useful over a longer time.

Key Points

Explaining your choice of methodology is essential if your project is to be credible. Reading and using the literature on doing research will provide important justifications for the choices and decisions you make.

How many methods should you choose?

My answer to this question is predictable, but perhaps not over-helpful: sufficient to collect data which answer your research questions. If pushed, I recommend (for a beginner researcher) using two or three different methods. These may gather either quantitative or qualitative data, or both – known as 'mixed' or 'combined' methods. If still in doubt, discuss it with your project tutor.

This does not mean that one method answers one research question, whilst another method answers another. You can and should think in more complicated ways than this. For instance, your interviews may provide data for two or more research questions; observations may provide data which help to answer all of them. It is also possible not to choose all your methods at the start, but to decide on them as your investigation develops. For instance, you carry out a questionnaire survey, examine the data produced, and only then decide what your next method should be. This cumulative process is often associated with a 'grounded-theory' approach (see Chapter 1).

'Sampling'

Choosing methods is not the only decision you have to make. You also need to decide who you will ask to participate in them. This process is called 'sampling', and the participants you choose are called your 'sample'. This sample represents what is known in turn as your 'population', that is all those to whom your research applies and who could theoretically (if you had time and resources) be participants in your investigation.

For instance, your investigation is about how students in a school view the teaching of modern foreign languages. You cannot interview all the students, so you choose a few – a sample – and talk with them. If you did a questionnaire with all students in that school, then your 'sample' for that aspect of your research would be the same as your 'population'.

There are different ways of approaching this sampling task. For instance:

- You can choose participants at random.
- You can select your participants because they have some kind of specialist expertise in the area you are investigating.
- You can select them because they represent certain groups, for example one or both genders, specific age groups, people with and without disabilities, relevant ethnic groups. You should only do this in ways which clearly relate to your topic and research questions. Otherwise, it would not be ethical to deny participants the opportunity to take part on the basis of such factors.
- You can ask someone else to select your participants.

 Three researchers adopt different approaches to sampling

- For her research on children's games, Bridget observes at random in the playground. She looks out for any interesting activity and writes down what she sees.
- Alison is investigating the reading habits of teenagers. For her questionnaires and interviews, she deliberately chooses an equal number of boys and girls, representatives of each of the main ethnic groups and students with varying examination grades. She feels that this will strengthen the balance and variety of the data she collects and allow her to make comparisons when she does her analysis (see Chapter 11).
- Toby is investigating opinions of very able students. For his interviews, he decides to ask the teacher to select from her class those she feels are the most advanced.

Also take into account these 'dos and don'ts' about choosing your sample:

- **Ask the right people:** For instance, if you wish to find out about students' views on the curriculum, ask the students themselves. Do not ask their teachers what they think students' views are.
- **Do not give work to others which you could do yourself:** For instance, if you wish to know what a policy document says, examine the document – do not ask others to tell you what it says.
- **Plan carefully the involvement of children and young people:** Their participation can be very valuable, but you must consider their welfare

at all times. For interviews, I recommend you involve them in groups, not individually. If you wish to focus on a particular individual, for instance for an in-depth case study (see Chapter 1), you should make sure that the student, the student's parents and the professionals involved understand what you are doing, give consent and are treated with respect throughout the research process.

- **Get consent**: Whatever approach you take, and whoever your participants are, you will need to inform them about your research and obtain their permission to be involved. We deal with this important ethical issue in Chapter 9.

Colin's project below outlines one approach to methodology. Note how he makes decisions on methods, samples and practicalities, and how the data he plans to collect will help to answer his research questions.

 ### Colin chooses his research methods

Colin is investigating how a primary school prepares its final-year students for transition to secondary schooling. His first research question asks what preparation strategies are used; his second asks what staff and students feel about these; his third focuses specifically on how coordination between the two schools is achieved. He decides on three research methods, supported by the literature on doing research which he has consulted:

1 **Questionnaires** to students will provide an overview of what they experienced and felt during transition. He decides he will ask all students now in their first year at the secondary school to complete the questionnaire. The data will help him to answer all of his research questions, especially question 2.

2 **Interviews** with teachers will provide more in-depth information, again for question 2 in particular. Interviews with the transition coordinators at both schools will provide specific data for question 3.

3 **Observation** of transition events will tell him about strategies in use and how they relate to his questionnaire and interview data, helping him to answer his first research question in particular.

Colin plans to carry out his investigation in the spring, when events to prepare for transition are taking place, and while students now at the secondary school can still recall their experiences from the previous year.

Project Sheet 8   Choosing methods

Project Sheet 8 in Appendix I provides a framework for making the same kind of decisions about your own research methodology. Complete one sheet for each of the methods you think you will use at this stage. Remember to read more about data-collection methods, using your course reading list and the further reading recommended here.

Completing Project Sheet 8 means you are ready to move on to the next stage: designing the tools – known as 'research instruments'– which you will use to collect your data from your chosen participants. This will form the basis of our next chapter.

Further reading

Burton, D. and Bartlett, S. (2005) *Practitioner Research for Teachers*. London: Sage.
Chapter 10 considers the kind of documentary material relating to schools which might be used in research, for instance policy documents, inspection reports, schemes of work and data about student achievement. It also looks at how such material can be analysed (we will also examine this in Chapter 11).

Cohen, L., Manion, L. and Morrison, K. (2011) *Research Methods in Education*. 7th ed. Abingdon: Routledge.
A substantial, much-reissued text with detailed coverage of a wide range of research methods.

David, M. and Sutton, C.D. (2011) *Social Research: An Introduction*. 2nd ed. London: Sage.
This book is for students taking a research methods course for the first time. It covers a range of approaches, including Internet research, mixed methods and grounded theory.

Ritchie, J. and Lewis, J. (eds) (2003) *Qualitative Research Practice: A Guide for Social Science Students and Researchers*. London: Sage.
Early chapters in this book deal clearly and thoughtfully with methods of collecting qualitative data, including sampling and ordering of data collection. Later parts will help you with the design of research instruments (which we address in our next chapter) and analysis of qualitative data (as we discuss in Chapter 11).

Roberts-Holmes, G. (2011) *Doing Your Early Years Project: A Step-by-Step Guide.* 2nd ed. London: Sage.
One chapter of this popular guide is entitled 'Creative Listening to Children', where the author considers how children's perspectives can be researched in verbal and visual ways, for instance through drawing, painting and photography.

 Methodspace: www.methodspace.com

Methodspace is an online network, hosted by Sage, for those engaged in research methods. Use it to network and share research, resources and ideas. It gives you free access to selected journal articles, book chapters and other material, representing emerging topics and debates in the field.

8 Designing your research instruments

What will you learn from this chapter?

In this chapter, we continue our focus on methodology and consider the design of your 'research instruments'. These are the tools and resources you will use to collect and record your data. Designing and using them well is crucial to the success of your project.

Research instruments (and ethics)

All research methods have some kind of research instrument (also called a 'data-collection instrument'), for instance:

- for **questionnaires**, it is the questionnaire itself
- for **interviews**, it is a list of questions which you plan to ask and how you will ask them: your 'interview framework'
- for **observations**, it is a chart or table which helps you to focus your attention on what you wish to observe and record what you see: an 'observation framework'
- for **document analysis**, it is the documents you choose to examine and the way in which you scrutinize them
- for **testing**, it is the test itself and the criteria by which it will be assessed.

Whatever research instruments you design, you will be incorporating within them two important ethical promises to your participants, both designed to protect them from possible embarrassment or harm when what they say, write or do is shared with others. These are:

- **Anonymity**: You should undertake to conceal the identity of your participants and anyone else mentioned in the data. This includes the name of your research venue, the educational setting where you do your investigation.
- **Confidentiality**: You should promise not to share original or 'raw' data from your research with others, only when those data have been analysed and anonymized.

There may be exceptions to these undertakings. For instance, you may need to share details of your research venue and original data with your project tutor or others who have a proper professional interest in your work. If this is the case, they too should respect your promises not to share information further than necessary. There can be occasions also when participants do not wish to remain anonymous – perhaps a school wishes its work to become better known through your research. If so, then you should respect these wishes, as long as they do not compromise the wishes of others.

The reason I raise these issues now is because you need to assure your participants about them in your research instruments. Now we look at each type of research instrument in turn and give guidance and examples of how these can be designed.

Designing questionnaires

In the last chapter, I warned that creating a questionnaire is difficult to do well. You must think very carefully about the questions you include and the way you present them, and you should be prepared to go through several versions until you get it right.

Questions to ask

Firstly, what questions should you include? There are two main types: closed and open.

Closed questions: Closed questions (sometimes called 'forced-choice questions') provide a range of answers from which your respondent must choose. Figure 8.1 gives some examples (Blaxter et al., 2010: 203, offer more).

As you can see, questions of this kind are fairly quick and easy to answer. First, they are good for getting factual data: *Are you male or female? Which*

Please indicate the extent to which you agree with this statement: 'Every child should start to learn a modern foreign language before the age of 11'.

Strongly agree	Largely agree	Not sure	Largely disagree	Strongly disagree

Which of the following vocational courses do you think should be offered in this college? Please tick all those that apply.

Hospitality   ☐

Interior design   ☐

Retail management   ☐

Food technology   ☐

Other (please specify) _____

Please place the following school facilities in order of preference (1 for the one you most enjoy using, 2 for your next favourite, and so on):

Recreational area   ☐

Library   ☐

Gym   ☐

Computer suite   ☐

Music room   ☐

Figure 8.1 Examples of closed questions

class are you in? For how many years have you worked as a teacher? Questions like this can be very useful, because (as we will see in Chapter 11) the responses you get allow you to examine how different groups respond to other questions you ask, for instance how answers from students from one class compare to those from another. You should therefore think carefully now about what questions of this kind you need to ask – what data you will need to answer your research questions. As we noted in the previous chapter, once your questionnaires are given out, you cannot change them to ask questions you forgot to include.

Closed questions also give you brief indications of preferences and opinions: *Which of the following options do you like most? How do you grade the usefulness of this resource?* The data you collect from such questions can be easily counted and analysed (see Chapter 11); however, the information is usually rather shallow and limited to options which you, the researcher, have provided. With closed questions, the respondent has few opportunities to offer different responses of their own.

Open questions: Open questions (sometimes called 'free-answer questions') allow respondents to think more independently and write at greater length about thoughts, opinions and experiences. They provide more data than closed questions, but take longer for respondents to answer and the data produced are harder to analyse (see Chapter 11). Here are some examples of open questions (note that some are the same as the closed questions listed above, but without choices set by the researcher):

- Please list the subjects you teach.
- What is your view of this statement?: 'Every child should start to learn a modern foreign language before the age of 11'.
- What do you use a computer for at home?
- What is your favourite subject at school? Explain the reasons for your choice.
- What do you understand by the term 'creative curriculum'?
- Any further comments on this issue?

Using closed and open questions

If your questionnaire only includes closed questions, you may be missing opportunities to gather important information. If it only contains open questions, the questionnaire will be arduous to complete and your respondents will be reluctant to tackle it. A good solution, therefore, is to include both. Here is some advice on how to do this:

- Start your questionnaire with some easy-to-answer, closed questions. These might ask for factual data, such as gender or professional role. These will help your respondents to get quickly into their task and could allow you to separate out the data you get into different groups (see Chapter 11).
- In closed questions use: *Other (please specify)* to give respondents the option of providing extra information – see the 'vocational courses' example in Figure 8.1. A 'not sure' box (see the question about modern foreign languages) can help respondents who are undecided about your issue; some researchers like a 'no opinion' column as well for respondents who have no view on the issue at all.
- In some cases, follow a closed with an open question, giving respondents opportunity to expand on their answer. For example: *Please explain your choice.*
- Always end your questionnaire with an open opportunity to write something more: *Any further comments which you wish to add?*

Questions to avoid

Whether you use closed or open questions or both, there are some styles of questions you should avoid:

1 Questions where the only possible answers are 'yes', 'no' or 'don't know' (unless you are seeking simple factual information). Use a rating scale (sometimes called a 'Likert scale') instead, as in the modern foreign languages question in Figure 8.1. Five or seven points on the scale, with a balance between positive and negative items, will give you much more varied and interesting data.

2 Questions where you could find out the information better from other sources, for example by looking at documents or asking other participants.

3 Unnecessary questions – for instance, do not ask for the age of respondents unless you really need to know.

4 Questions which appear to test the knowledge or competence of your respondents (unless you state clearly that this is what you wish to do).

5 Questions which are simply too vague or broad to answer well.

6 Double questions, where two or more questions are rolled into one.

7 Complex, ambiguous or 'loaded' questions.

8 Questions with poor spelling or grammar.

 Activity 8.1   Questions to avoid

Why are the questions below unsuitable? Match them against the list above (some are unsuitable for more than one reason). Suggested answers are in Appendix II.

A Why is it important for children to play competitive sport?

B What does your school development plan say about playground facilities?

C Do children have regular opportunities to read in your class?

D Are you married and do you have children?

E Do students think reading is OK?

F What are the causes of boys' underachievement in school?

G Why don't students pay attention if they sit at the back and can't see you and how do you deal with that when or if it happens?

H What is the meaning of education?

Setting out your questions

No matter how good your questions are, your respondents will only answer them well if they are presented clearly in your questionnaire. Here are some suggestions for doing this effectively:

Titles: Provide clear titles at the start. For example:

**Investigating the use of non-fiction texts
in the teaching of English**
*Research project by Mike Lambert for BA in Education,
University of Nowhere
Questionnaire for teachers*

Introduction: Include an initial thank you and short instructions. For example: *Thank you for agreeing to complete this questionnaire. The questions ask about your experiences and opinions of breakfast clubs. Please tick the relevant boxes, or write your answers in the spaces provided.*

Closed questions: Use Table, Tab and Aligning functions on your computer to ensure that the layout of questions and boxes is well organized. State clearly what you wish respondents to do – for example to tick one box, or all boxes that apply, or list items in order of preference. Be consistent where possible – for instance, do not ask respondents to tick an option in one question, then to circle an option in the next.

Open questions: Indicate how much you would like respondents to write. You can request this directly, for example: *Please give three reasons for your answer*, or you can provide an appropriate space or number of lines for the response.

Designing for children: There are several ways of making a questionnaire more age-appropriate for children: simpler language, a less formal style, use of icons (like smiley faces) in place of statements. Take care, however, not to underestimate children's abilities – overdoing a child-friendly style can diminish the sense of responsibility they get from participating. If you are present when they complete their questionnaires, you have the option to give additional verbal explanations.

Conclusion: A date of completion (not a signature so as to respect anonymity), another thank you and an instruction about what to do next are sufficient to round things off: *Thank you for completing this questionnaire. Please return it in the envelope provided to the school office – I will collect it from there.*

Other suggestions on presentation:

- Use an uncomplicated, easy-to-read font, for example Arial, Tahoma, Times New Roman or Comic Sans Relief.
- Use both italics and standard lettering in a logical way. For example, write instructions in italics and the questions themselves in standard lettering.
- Check the questionnaire closely for mistakes and ask a friend to check as well.
- I suggest a maximum length of four sides of A4. Printing pages back-to-back will make your questionnaire look more compact and less onerous to complete.

Project Sheet 9   Designing a questionnaire

If you plan to use a questionnaire, start to design it now, using the guidance above, your wider reading and Project Sheet 9 in Appendix I. Think about structure and layout, and mix closed and open questions in your design. The Project Sheet is a guide only – you should decide how many closed and open questions you wish to ask and in what order to do so. Your questionnaire should be easy for respondents to complete, but also give you useful data – this is a difficult balance to achieve.

Designing interviews

As with questionnaires, interview design must lead to useful data which help to answer the research questions you set at the start of your project. For a 30-minute, semi-structured interview, think in terms of asking your interviewees between three and eight main questions, and list these in your 'interview framework'.

Structure

A key element to consider is structure. My recommendation involves four stages: introduction, simple start, meaty middle and rounding off at the end.

1 **Introduction:** Introduce yourself and explain your research in a couple of sentences. Thank your interviewee for participating and remind them how you will use the data they provide. For example: *My name*

is Mike Lambert. As you know, I am researching the use of online history resources at this school. Thank you for agreeing to this interview. I will treat what you say confidentially and will not identify you by name in my written project or elsewhere. If you do not wish to answer a question, please say so and we will move on to another.

2 **Simple start:** Your first questions should act as 'icebreakers', relaxing the interviewee and getting them talking. This is also a good opportunity to obtain any basic information you need. For example:

- *Can you first tell me a little about your professional background?*
- *What are your curricular responsibilities at this school?*
- *Thank you for letting me observe your lesson yesterday. What did you feel about how the students completed their tasks?*

3 **Meaty middle:** The middle of your interview is the longest and most important part. Here you deepen the conversation, focusing closely on specific aspects which you wish to explore. Here are some examples of the kind of data you can seek:

- Deeper factual information: *What has the college done to address government changes in the curriculum?*
- Opinions: *What are your views on these changes?*
- Evaluations: *From your perspective, what are the advantages of this teaching approach? What are the disadvantages?*
- Recollection of a significant event: *What triggered this student's exclusion from school?*
- Recollection of experiences: *How did your own practice change as a result of these events?*
- Comments on an observed occurrence: *Why did you recall the students to their tables at this point?*
- Intentions: *How will you deal with this difficulty in future lessons?*
- Hypothetical perspectives: *What would you do if this happened again?*

4 **Rounding off:** Your last question should be an invitation to say more: *Do you have anything further to say on this topic?* Finally, of course, thank your interviewee and assure them that their input will be very useful for your research.

How to interview

Another part of your interview planning is working out how to interview, so here are more factors to consider:

Digging deep: Interviews are not simply about asking questions and listening to answers. You should 'actively engage with [interviewees], often thinking on [your] feet' (Barbour and Schostak, 2005: 45). You should prompt, probe, seek reasons, explanations and examples – in short, you 'dig deep'. Here, for example, are some of the supplementary questions you should be asking:

- *Can you clarify what you mean?*
- *That is interesting – please tell me more.*
- *Can you give me an example of that?*
- *Have you experienced that situation yourself? What happened and how did you deal with it?*

You can also express a lack of knowledge or an opposite view to stimulate discussion:

- *I have not heard of that before – can you explain?*
- *That is not a common opinion – how do you justify it?*
- *What would you say to those who take a different view?*

 Key Points

Interviews allow you to explore issues and opinions in depth – but this only happens if you make it happen. Be curious, delve, dig deep!

Interviewing groups: Interviewing two or more people together means that new ideas can be sparked off between them – this can be particularly valuable in exploratory research. Beware, however, that some interviewees may dominate, whilst others are hesitant about expressing their views. You need to give everyone a turn, but also allow individual speakers to explain their perspectives in reasonable detail (another difficult balance to achieve). Note too that confidentiality can be compromised in a group – you should instruct participants not to disclose what is said beyond the context of the interview discussion.

Interviewing children: If your group interviews are with children, you may need to simplify questions and find alternatives for adult-oriented terminology. Be extra careful not to 'lead' their responses – some may easily be tempted to say what they think you, the adult, wants to hear. The positive side is that most children enjoy being interviewed, especially if you spice up the discussion with a task, perhaps choosing favourites from a list, or discussing hypothetical situations. It can also be effective if you appear to lack understanding (which may be true) and ask for explanation. Lofland et al. (2006: 46) called this 'a "learner" or "incompetent" role', but also warned too about pushing it too far – you should at least appear reasonably capable as a researcher.

Recording what is said: One difficult decision is how to keep a record of what is said. Even with short interviews, you cannot rely on memory – you need proper evidence which you can analyse later. There are two main possibilities for this: voice recording or taking written notes. Let us look at the pluses and minuses of each.

On the plus side, voice recording will leave you free to listen and discuss during the interview itself and give you an exact account of what was said. Transcribing your recording will help you to get to know your data, but will take a long time (approximately one hour of work for every 5–10 minutes of recorded speech). Participants (adults, usually, rather than children) may regard the process as intrusive and not wish to be recorded in this way.

Written notes, on the other hand, will not need transcription (although you may wish to type them up) and will be more generally acceptable to interviewees. However, you may find it hard to write during the interview, it may be difficult to decide what to write and what to ignore, and ultimately you may feel that your notes appear sparse or incomplete.

It is possible to lessen the difficulties associated with each approach. For instance, with voice recordings, rather than transcribing every word, listen closely to the recording and take written notes from this, including direct quotations which illuminate or exemplify particular ideas. If you take written notes, find ways of abbreviating what you write ('chn' for children, 'sts' for students, etc.) and practise writing in this way beforehand. As soon as you can after the interview, make legible any scribble and use your memory to enhance your notes further. Another possibility, if you can manage it, is to enlist a third person who takes notes at the interview for you. You will need to explain this extra presence to your interviewee and make sure that this third person makes the same promises on confidentiality which you have provided.

Project Sheet 10   Interview framework

Using the guidance above and Project Sheet 10 (Appendix I), list your main questions, considering carefully the order of asking them. Indicate also how you intend to carry out the interview. When complete, use these questions to design a chart for taking notes during the interview or from the voice recording.

Designing observations

Decisions about observations largely match those for other methods above: What to observe? How to record? And most importantly: Will the data I collect help to answer my research questions?

What to observe?

For an educational project, the most likely place for observation is the classroom. There are other possibilities too, for example meetings or places where there is interaction between people and the physical environment, such as the extent to which college facilities are accessible to a student with a disability. In any situation, deciding who or what exactly to observe can be problematic. For instance, it is probably impossible to observe a whole class of students – you simply cannot see and record all the interactions taking place. In most situations, therefore, you need to work out exactly what or who to observe: a group of students, an individual, the teacher, specific events, or a combination of these.

How much to observe?

Another decision to take is how much to observe. Here are some possibilities:

- **Continuous**: You observe activity continuously, for instance everything which a group of students does throughout a lesson. Doing this could result in large amounts of data, some of which may not be useful for your research.
- **Periodic or interval**: You observe intensively for one minute, then take a two-minute break (or whatever time ratio you decide). Or at set intervals, for instance every three minutes, you note down what those you are observing are doing and ignore what they do between those times.
- **Event-sampling**: You watch continuously, but only record something when you see it happen. For instance, you note down every time you see evidence of a student's misconception or lack of understanding. You can count such instances or describe them, or both.

Recording observations

As with interviews, you need to decide how you will record your data. You could, for instance:

- take continuous written notes about what you see and hear
- keep a tally chart to count how many times something happens

- draw a map of the room and use it to track movements of students or staff
- do a combination of these, relevant to what you wish to find out (Hopkins, 2008, provides further examples).

You might also consider video recording. This will provide a permanent record which you can watch many times and analyse in detail, possibly in discussion with those you have filmed. The practical disadvantages are, however, quite substantial:

- It may be complicated and difficult to get agreement from all those you are filming.
- With a moveable camera, you will need to make instant decisions about what to film.
- With a fixed camera, where do you place it? Will you capture what you wish to see?

In this light, my general advice for beginner researchers is not to use video filming, but to observe and take written notes personally instead. If you think differently, read up on what is involved (for instance, S. Robson, 2011), and discuss the possibility with your project tutor.

Observation framework

The complications of observation make it very important that you prepare some kind of chart or framework in advance, so you can organize the notes you take. Here are some possible designs for this:

- **Continuous record**: You wish to take notes on interactions between teacher and students, so your chart has the following columns:
  a 'Time': for noting the time at regular intervals
  b 'Teacher behaviour': for writing down what the teacher does and says
  c 'Student behaviour': for recording what students do and say
  d 'Notes': for other relevant notes.

- **Tallying**: To count how many times particular events take place, your columns might be rather simpler:
  a 'Event': the nature of the event you observe
  b 'Timing': when it happens
  c 'Tally': counting how many times it happens
  d 'Comments': any further relevant notes.
- **Shorthand**: Observer researchers sometimes design a shorthand system to quicken note-taking and facilitate later analysis. For this, you need to identify the aspects of the observation which you wish

to record, and give each of these some kind of abbreviation or symbol. Note how Jenny does this below.

Jenny devises a shorthand system for recording teacher–student interactions

Jenny is interested in verbal interactions between teacher and students, but realizes that she cannot write down everything which is said in a busy classroom. She therefore devises a more concise system (she has seen how past researchers have done this, for instance Galton et al., 1980). She decides to use three elements, abbreviated with letters:

- Her first letter denotes the person making an utterance.
- Her second letter describes the nature of the utterance, for example an instruction or suggestion.
- Her third letter identifies the listener to what is said.

So 'TQC' indicates that the teacher (T) asks a question (Q) to the whole class (C); 'SRC' that one student (S) gives a response (R) which is audible to the whole class (C). 'TLC' indicates that the teacher (T) has set a time limit (L) to the class (C): 'You have five minutes to complete your work'; 'SPS2' that a student (S) refers to previous learning (P) to two other students (S2): 'We did this yesterday'. She tests this system and, as a result, adds more abbreviations to her list. On the whole, it seems to work – she can keep a written record of whole-class and group interactions and sometimes even has time to scribble down the exact words spoken by the teacher and students during the lesson.

Project Sheet 11   Observation framework

Project Sheet 11 in Appendix I encourages you to state the focus of each of your observations, its type, how you will carry it out and the context in which it takes place, for instance nature of classroom, age and number of students. After that, the kind of framework you design will depend on what and how you wish to observe. Use the guidance in this chapter to adapt the chart, so that headings match the nature of your observation and so you can use it for taking your notes.

Preparing for document analysis

The main preparation for document analysis is to decide which documents to look at. We listed some possibilities in Chapter 7 – what you actually choose is your sample. It is important that you have permission to examine these, and extra permission if you wish to copy them or take them away. Promises of confidentiality and anonymity may need to be provided too. You will read your chosen documents closely, annotating the text itself or by making separate notes – we look at this process of analysis in Chapter 11.

Designing tests

In the previous chapter, I also listed the kinds of tests which might be used in research, either those already published or one of your own. If the latter, remember that designing tests and comparing the results obtained is a specialist business, so keep yours short and simple. If it is a written or spoken test, you may prefer to use closed rather than open questions or tasks, not least because these are easier to assess. Whatever approach you take, always make sure that your respondents are happy for you to test them in this way.

In what order do I use my methods?

There is one more question to consider, which applies to your methodology as a whole: in what order should you carry out your methods? This is an important decision – you increase the value of your methods by combining them or relating one to another. Here are some possibilities:

- You could use questionnaires first to get an overview of key issues from a large sample, then use the resulting data as a basis for more in-depth questioning of individuals in interview.
- You could carry out interviews after observation, so you can evaluate aspects of the lesson with your interviewee.
- You could analyse policy documents to find out the aims or intentions of an institution, then carry out observations to see if these are confirmed or contradicted in practical situations.

Well on your way

In this chapter, we have looked at how to design research instruments so you collect detailed, useful data. Does that mean you are ready to start your investigation? Sadly, not quite. There are more decisions to make in the next chapter, but with your methods chosen and research instruments set out in draft, you are certainly well on your way.

Further reading 📖

Drever, E. (1995) *Using Semi-Structured Interviews in Small-Scale Research: A Teacher's Guide.* Glasgow: Scottish Council for Research in Education.
A concise guide to this form of interviewing, the kind you are most likely to use.

Punch, K.F. (2003) *Survey Research: The Basics.* London: Sage.
For me, this is the most accessible guide to designing and using questionnaires to collect quantitative data. It will help you design and implement an effective questionnaire.

Rubin, H.J. and Rubin, I.S. (2005) *Qualitative Interviewing: The Art of Hearing Data.* 2nd ed. London: Sage.
This is my favourite text on interviewing. As the cover says, it explains 'how to obtain rich, detailed and evocative information through open-ended, in-depth interviewing' – what I have called 'digging deep'.

Wragg, E.C. (1999) *An Introduction to Classroom Observation.* 2nd ed. Abingdon: Routledge.
Some of the content may now seem a little dated, but Ted Wragg's book, written for teachers rather than researchers, remains a valuable guide to skills of observation which capture what in the preface the author calls 'the familiarity and novelty' of classroom activity.

9 Validity, reliability and ethical approval

What will you learn from this chapter?

This chapter helps you to strengthen the data you collect from your methods and data-collection instruments by discussing the important issues of validity and reliability. We also consider how you apply for 'ethical approval' from your place of study to carry out your research. By the end of the chapter, you will be ready to find or confirm your research venue and carry out your investigation.

Threats to objectivity

We have already mentioned (in Chapter 5) the need for objectivity when doing research. This is not easy to achieve: think of some of the situations which might lead you astray:

- You work in the same profession as your research participants, so you feel you already know how they think.
- Your participants are work colleagues or friends. Your research could produce unwelcome findings, but to protect their feelings, you do not explore these negative aspects too closely.
- You already have your own opinions on your topic – you feel that your research is a good way of expressing these views.

These situations are not compatible with a wholly objective approach to research. Indeed, some would argue that objectivity is impossible to achieve completely – researchers are human beings with feelings and these unavoidably influence their investigation. However, maintaining a sense of neutrality is part of your role as a researcher, in the face of many threats to it. Here are some other situations which could affect the balance of your investigation:

'Hawthorne effect': Early in the last century, experiments were carried out at the Hawthorne Electrical Works in the USA. The researcher, Elton Mayo, concluded that workers' performance improved simply because they were being investigated. This phenomenon became known as the 'Hawthorne effect'. It means that your research may itself change people's behaviour – for instance, students' performance may look rosier than would be the case if you were not doing your investigation.

Loaded questions: Your questions may unintentionally presume a certain kind of answer. Consider this very simple example: 'What do you enjoy about school?'. It presumes that your respondents enjoy school, a 'loaded' question unless you balance it by asking the opposite: 'What don't you enjoy?' as well. Question A in Activity 8.1 in the previous chapter was also loaded in this way.

Irregular samples: You send a questionnaire to parents, but some do not speak English as their first language and therefore do not complete your questionnaire. Your data will be biased towards those who know English well.

Activity 9.1   Threats to objectivity

With colleagues, identify and discuss other possible threats to balanced research, relating, for instance, to:

- choice of samples
- poorly designed questions
- external influences, including your own prior experiences and opinions.

All this may sound rather depressing. If objectivity is so difficult, perhaps research is not worth doing at all. The answer is two-fold:

- In your investigation, you should identify and examine threats to objectivity and be prepared to write about them in your written project.
- Take reasonable steps also to reduce those threats – we will consider some possible actions you can take later in this chapter.

Note that I have not talked about 'eliminating threats' or 'achieving objectivity'. As we noted, it is doubtful that research can ever be fully objective or free from bias. Your task as a researcher is to be conscious of difficulties and to reduce the ways in which they might affect your investigation.

Jack and Jill's unbalanced data

Jack is carrying out several group interviews with children. He finds out early on that girls tend to contribute more to discussion than boys; and confident, lucid children more than shyer ones. Jill has done a questionnaire with college students – she found that those who were good at English wrote more than those who were not, and older students wrote more than younger ones. Jack and Jill both realize that their data are biased towards the views of the groups who have spoken or written more and not sufficiently balanced with those who have spoken or written less. Jack resolves to do more in subsequent interviews to encourage quieter children, especially boys, to speak. Jill decides to examine her imbalances when she analyses her data and writes up her project.

Rohan evaluates a course for very able students

Rohan is evaluating a three-week, out-of-school course for very able students. In the final week, he gives them a questionnaire asking for their views of the course. He realizes, however, that the data will not include the views of students who left part-way through – his research is biased in favour of those who attended until the end. He decides to try and contact those who dropped out so that they can complete the questionnaire as well. He resolves also to point out this issue in his written project.

Validity and reliability

There are two important concepts in research which relate to this whole issue: 'validity' and 'reliability'. You may have already come across these in your reading on research. We will consider each in turn now, then examine how you can address them.

Validity

I want to measure how tall I am. My friend gives me some bathroom scales: 'Measure yourself with these'. 'I can't', I reply. 'Scales are for measuring weight. They are not a valid instrument for measuring height.'

My friend wants to measure how heavy he is. I give him a measuring tape: 'Weigh yourself with this'. 'I can't', he replies. 'A tape is for measuring length and height. It is not a valid instrument for measuring weight.'

 Key Points

Validity is the extent to which an instrument measures what it is supposed to measure. Put another way, it is the extent to which an instrument helps a researcher to find out what she or he wishes to find out.

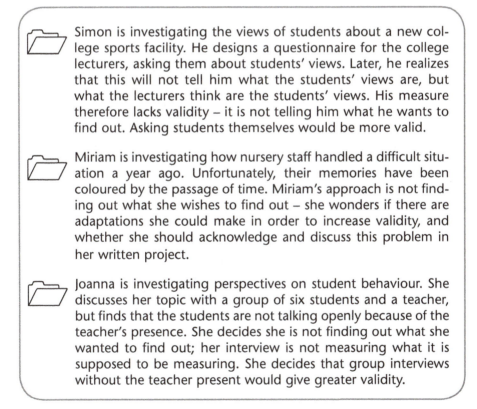

Simon is investigating the views of students about a new college sports facility. He designs a questionnaire for the college lecturers, asking them about students' views. Later, he realizes that this will not tell him what the students' views are, but what the lecturers think are the students' views. His measure therefore lacks validity – it is not telling him what he wants to find out. Asking students themselves would be more valid.

Miriam is investigating how nursery staff handled a difficult situation a year ago. Unfortunately, their memories have been coloured by the passage of time. Miriam's approach is not finding out what she wishes to find out – she wonders if there are adaptations she could make in order to increase validity, and whether she should acknowledge and discuss this problem in her written project.

Joanna is investigating perspectives on student behaviour. She discusses her topic with a group of six students and a teacher, but finds that the students are not talking openly because of the teacher's presence. She decides she is not finding out what she wanted to find out; her interview is not measuring what it is supposed to be measuring. She decides that group interviews without the teacher present would give greater validity.

Reliability

I want to measure the length of a piece of wood, using a valid instrument: a tape measure. Unfortunately, the tape measure is of poor quality and stretches in warm weather. It therefore gives me different results according to the time of year. My tape measure is not a reliable instrument for measuring length.

I want to weigh a bag of sugar, using some kitchen scales. Every time I put this bag on the scales, I get the same result: one kilogram. If I remove half a kilo from the bag, my scales say that what is left weighs half a kilo too. Use of my scales seems to be a reliable method for weighing my bag of sugar.

 **Key Points**

> Reliability means that a method is free from error. When it is used repeatedly, it produces consistent results.

Here are examples of this concept, applied to research:

- I give 50 children a questionnaire. One of my questions is ambiguous – some children interpret it one way, others in another. This question lacks reliability – it does not produce consistent results. It will be very difficult for me to collate and analyse responses.

- I plan to interview two teachers and compare the views expressed. For one interview, I find a quiet room, free from distraction. For the other, I grab a few minutes in a busy classroom and talk there. My comparison will lack reliability because I have not given my interviewees similar opportunities to express their views.

- I am counting occasions when students keep or do not keep safety rules in science lessons. Before my first observation, I forget to find out exactly which safety rules the students are expected to follow. For my second, I am better prepared – I know the rules and can tell whether students abide by them or not. My comparison will have low reliability because my two observations were done in different ways.

In these examples, where the intention is to collate or compare answers, I should have sought greater consistency in my approach. This is not always the case, however. Sometimes we simply want to explore an issue from a variety of perspectives, not make comparisons, and in these cases we should not take the concept of reliability too far. For instance, because your interviewees have different professional roles, you may wish to structure their interviews differently, ask different questions, or spend longer with one than another. The focus of observations may fluctuate, reflecting your wish to find out different things. Qualitative data are often collected in varied ways, allowing you to explore in depth and build up rich data for analysis – the concept of reliability may not be applicable in these situations.

Strengthening validity and reliability

You should take steps to strengthen the validity and (where appropriate) the reliability of your investigation. Note my use of the word 'strengthen', not 'achieve'. This is because no matter how thorough you are, you will never reach complete validity and reliability in your research – simply too many other factors will be influencing what you do (I said the same thing about 'achieving objectivity' earlier). You should talk and write about the validity and reliability of your own project in a cautious way.

There are many things you can do to strengthen validity and reliability. Increasing the size of your sample is not one of these. Whether you involve three people or 300, if your approach is not measuring what you wish to measure, or lacks consistency, your data will remain low in both of these qualities. Let us deal with three strategies which will strengthen these aspects of your research: triangulation, piloting and (a double concept we mentioned at the start of the previous chapter) anonymity and confidentiality.

Triangulation

You want to buy a new computer. You ask a few friends what they recommend and check some online reviews as well. Getting several opinions helps you reach a good decision. This is triangulation – using more than one method or more than one source to enhance the information you get (note that it does not mean using three approaches, just using more than one). For instance, in research terms:

- You use both questionnaires and interviews to gather opinions of a teaching approach.
- You interview teachers, students and parents so that all these viewpoints contribute to the picture you obtain.

 **Key Points**

> Triangulation means drawing data from two or more methods or sources, so that you can use a range of information to answer your research questions. In addition, weaknesses of one method or source may be compensated by strengths of another, so you can have greater confidence in what you find out.

'Piloting'

Piloting means testing out your methods and research instruments in advance and changing them as a result, usually by giving them some kind of 'practice run'. For instance:

- **Questionnaires**: You design a questionnaire to give to a class of children. You pilot it first with a few other children from elsewhere in the school. When this pilot group has completed it, you ask them: Was anything unclear or confusing? You check their written responses: Did they all understand the questions in the way you intended? You make changes based on what you discover (and keep a record of these alterations so you can explain them in your written project). You then give your improved questionnaire to the full class of children to complete.
- **Interviews**: You plan to use interviews. You first ask your interview questions to friends or colleagues and invite them to tell you the extent to which they understand them and how they could be improved. You keep a record of any changes you make as a result.
- **Observations**: You decide to test out your observation framework by doing a trial observation first. You use this experience to identify weaknesses in your observation design and improve your approach.

Piloting is especially important if others are helping you to collect your data. For instance, if you and a colleague are observing separate lessons, you should both observe the same lesson first and compare the notes you take. Did you see, interpret and record events in the same way? Iron out inconsistencies before starting your real observations. This issue is relevant to any method carried out by more than one researcher and is called 'inter-rater' or 'inter-observer' reliability.

Anonymity and confidentiality

We first met these concepts in relation to ethics in the previous chapter, but they can strengthen validity and reliability as well. By providing these assurances, you make it more likely that participants will give honest answers to your questions, particularly when talking about sensitive or difficult issues.

One aspect of this is to keep any data you collect securely so they do not fall into the wrong hands. For instance:

- Keep electronic data on a password-protected computer; keep paper data under lock and key.
- Change names and details as soon as you can – keep a separate and secure record of identities if needed for your own use.
- Do not use a memory stick to back up data (easily mislaid and looked at by others) – use a central server or other password-protected facility instead.
- Delete or destroy raw data when you no longer need them.

 Project sheet 12   Validity and reliability

Use Project Sheet 12 in Appendix I to identify three threats to objectivity in your project. Use the ideas in this chapter to work out what these might be. Then state three steps you will take to strengthen the validity and reliability of your research, again using the suggestions given in this chapter.

Ethical approval

Your research is planned, you are ready to collect data. There is (probably) one more very important task to do: ask your place of study for 'ethical approval' to carry out your investigation. This is when those responsible for your studies assess and confirm your readiness to carry out your research in ways which respect the rights and needs of your participants. Exact procedures will differ from one institution to another, so you should take steps to clarify your own position.

There are a number of issues to consider as part of this process. We have already looked at two of these: your promises to participants about anonymity and confidentiality. Now we discuss three more: 'informed consent', dealing with sensitive and difficult data, and researching with children and other vulnerable groups.

Informed consent

Informed consent means two things: that those involved one way or another in your research understand the nature of your investigation, and that they agree to take part on this basis.

Telling people about your research

The first step, therefore, is informing people about your research. There are two groups you should tell: those you hope will contribute (questionnaire respondents, interviewees, those you wish to observe), and those who have professional or personal responsibility for them. This latter group may include the headteacher or principal, parents or carers. They are known in the research literature as 'gatekeepers', because they decide whether to let you have access to others (staff, children) for whom they are responsible.

You can tell potential participants and their gatekeepers about your investigation verbally, in writing, or both. I suggest both: talk about your research (see Activity 9.2), but also have a simple written summary to give to anyone involved. This summary is your 'research brief' and we will consider how you can draw it up at the end of this chapter.

 Activity 9.2   Can you talk clearly about your research?

> In two sentences, describe accurately the topic of your research and what you wish to find out. Test your ability to do this by talking with a friend or colleague. Invite them to ask you further questions as well: 'Why did you choose this topic?'; 'How will you gather data?' Good researchers can talk concisely and clearly about their investigation – this is your chance to find out if you can do so.

Who gives consent?

When people understand your research, you can ask for their consent to take part. This sounds fairly straightforward, but it is not. For instance, a mature teenager can give consent, but do their parents (their gatekeepers) have to agree too? What about a child of 10, or 7, or 4, or a child with learning difficulties – to what extent can they give you their own informed agreement to take part? The literature on research with children often discusses such dilemmas (see, for instance, Masson, 2004, and Hill, 2005). For beginner researchers, my view is this: make everyone (gatekeepers and participants) aware of your research and give everyone the chance to withhold their consent if they so wish.

Types of consent

The process of getting consent is not always as onerous as it sounds. This is because there are two main types of consent:

- **Active consent**: This is where a participant actively agrees to take part. They tell you directly or sign a consent form.
- **Presumed or passive consent**: This is a simpler approach. You tell your participants about your research and ask them to indicate to you if they do not wish to participate. If they say nothing, you 'presume' they agree to participate.

Opinions on which approach is appropriate vary, so I recommend that you find out what your project tutor thinks, or what your course requirements might stipulate in this respect. My own view is that for beginner research, 'presumed consent' is usually sufficient. For instance, you inform parents that you will be observing children as part of your research, and simply ask them to contact you if they have any queries or concerns. Or you give out copies of your questionnaire at a staff meeting – if someone fills it in and returns it to you, you presume consent to use their data; if they do not, then their consent is withheld.

Active consent (for instance, by signing a form) may be needed in more complicated circumstances, for instance if:

- your topic is sensitive or contentious
- your research will cause major disruption to participants' normal routine
- you wish to film or photograph participants – children or adults (your research venue may already have permissions, which you should examine)

- you wish to research participants' home circumstances, family history or other personal issues
- your research will focus in depth on an individual child, student or other participant, for instance in a case study (see Chapter 1), or on particularly 'vulnerable' participants such as children in care (I discuss this issue of 'vulnerable groups' below).

Menter et al. (2011: 58–59) provide examples of a form you could use in situations like this. You may need to show the form you intend to use when applying for your ethical approval.

Note that even when you get consent, this does not oblige participants to take part in the whole of your research. They may not wish to answer a particular question you ask, or to take part in a particular activity or they could even withdraw altogether half way through. Ethically, you cannot object, although you can check how you might remove the obstacles or objections to their participation.

Dealing with sensitive and difficult data

We mentioned earlier that there are exceptions to the basic principles of anonymity and confidentiality, for instance the possibility that you will need to share data or identities with your project tutor. There are other, more serious occasions (fortunately very rare) where you cannot, and should not, keep confidential what is said to you during your research. What if, for instance:

- in a questionnaire, a child indicates that they might be suffering some kind of harm at home?
- during an interview, a participant tells you information suggesting criminal activity at a school or college?
- during an observation, you see a teacher striking a child?

These seem very unlikely, and they are. Even so, you should give some thought to what, if they happened, you would do.

At your research venue, there will be policies and procedures relating to difficult situations such as these. Most will involve sharing information about what has happened with a designated member of staff. For you as a researcher, this will mean breaking the promise of confidentiality which you gave to your participants. The three case studies below explore aspects of this important issue. The application form for ethical approval may require you to comment on such possibilities, and on the actions you would take if they occurred.

Devika decides that she must share sensitive information

While Devika is interviewing a small group of children, one makes an unusual comment which suggests that he may be suffering neglect or abuse at home. Devika decides that she must follow school policy in this case. First, she warns the child that she cannot keep confidential what he has said and must share the information with a senior teacher. The child continues nevertheless to make sensitive disclosures. After the interview, in accordance with school policy, Devika writes down what has happened and reports it to the school's designated child-protection teacher. Devika takes no further action herself and does not use the data collected from this child in her research study.

Adele decides not to share sensitive information given in confidence

In an interview, a student describes the personal difficulties his college work is causing for him at home. Adele encourages the student to talk through the problem with staff, but does not share it further herself. Another student, responding to Adele's questionnaire, indicates some distress with a piece of work she recently had to complete. Adele again does not share this information further. She feels that neither situation should override the assurance of confidentiality which she has given to her participants.

Chris sees a member of staff reacting aggressively to a child's misbehaviour

Chris is observing in the nursery playground. He sees a child being rude to one of the adult supervisors. This adult pulls the child across the playground and into the school. Chris knows that the adult's action is not permissible under the school's behaviour policy. He decides that he must discuss what he saw carefully and in confidence with a senior member of staff.

Activity 9.3   What would you do?

Discuss these three situations. Was each researcher correct in their response? What would you have done? On what other occasions might you need to break the promises of anonymity and confidentiality you give to your participants?

 Key Points

The way you handle the data you collect should in nearly all cases respect the promises of confidentiality and anonymity you gave to those who have contributed these data. However, concern for the greater safety and welfare of your participants, particularly children, may on very rare occasions override the promises you make.

Researching with children and other vulnerable groups

Finally, we need to consider issues relating specifically to research with children, students and other 'vulnerable groups'.

Power

As an adult and educator, you often tell children and students what to do (learn this, act like that) and you expect them to do as you say. You may not always feel very 'powerful', but if you think about it, you are. Researchers are in a similar position of authority – after all, you set your topic and you set the agenda for investigating it. Oliver (2010: 5) provided a simple principle which guards against the researcher's unfair exploitation of this position: 'The researcher is no more important than the person providing data; they merely have different roles'.

'Vulnerable' groups

Some groups are particularly susceptible to unequal relationships – in research they are known as 'vulnerable groups'. They include children and young people, in particular those:

* with learning difficulties or other disability
* with physical or mental illness

- in care, often termed 'looked-after'
- experiencing, or who have recently experienced, difficult social, cultural or political situations (for example, refugee children), or emotional trauma, such as bereavement, harassment or abuse.

Some of these categories may also relate to adults taking part in your research. Further, it is possible that participants not belonging to such groups could be 'made vulnerable' by your research. For instance, if you interview teachers about problems in a school and do not take proper steps to maintain anonymity, these teachers may be 'made vulnerable' to disciplinary censure for what they say.

It is possible that as a beginner researcher you will be allowed to involve participants from vulnerable groups in your research, or to carry out an investigation which could place participants in vulnerable positions. However, if you are seeking ethical approval for this kind of investigation, you should:

- discuss the ethical implications both with your tutor and at your research venue
- plan in detail how you will respect participants' welfare when doing your research
- follow special procedures to explain your research to participants, get their consent and protect their identity.

 Key Points

Your research is (rightly) important to you. However, you must not let this feeling override your respect and concern for those who take part (or who choose not to take part) in it. Take very seriously your responsibilities towards the welfare of your participants, and be respectful in the way you plan and carry out your investigation.

 Project Sheet 13   Ethics checklist

Project Sheet 13 in Appendix I lists the main ethical issues you should be considering at this stage of your project. Identify the steps you are taking to protect your participants and yourself from harm or disadvantage in relation to each of these issues.

Your research brief

Your project plan is formulated – you are now in a position to draw up your research brief. This is a summary which you can give to anyone who needs or wants to know about your research. You can attach it to any letter asking for access or consent and include it as an appendix in your written project. It should be:

- concise and informative
- clearly written, using language which participants (including children if possible) will understand
- grammatically accurate (a badly composed text will cast doubt on your competency)
- formal in style
- ideally one page long, and never longer than two.

What should it say?

Your research brief should include the following information:

1 Title

2 Who you are

3 The topic of your research

4 What you intend to do

5 How you intend to do it

6 How you will protect anonymity and confidentiality

7 What you will do with the data you collect

8 A timescale for your investigation

9 What kind of ethical approval you have received to carry out your research

10 Other information about relevant checks which allow you access to children and young people

11 How you will share the outcomes of your research

12 Your contact details, so that concerns or questions can be raised with you directly.

Project Sheet 14   Research brief

Monica is investigating the use of classroom routines with young children. Her research brief is Project Sheet 14 in Appendix I. First, identify in her text each of the numbered elements listed above. Then use it as a guide for drawing up a research brief of your own.

When complete, your research brief should be available in both printed and electronic formats. For the printed version, use coloured paper so it catches the eye. Note that if you are involving in your research families who have difficulty understanding English, you should at least write clearly and simply, and you might need to arrange either for your research brief to be translated, or for your investigation to be explained by other means.

Ready to go

You are now ready to find or confirm the venue for your research, to seek informed consent from potential participants and to undertake your investigation. All your careful preparation and planning will now bear fruit – you are ready to go.

Further reading 📖

Harcourt, D., Perry, B. and Waller, T. (eds) (2011) *Researching Young Children's Perspectives: Debating the Ethics and Dilemmas of Educational Research with Young Children.* London: Routledge.
This book examines challenges and ethical dilemmas which researchers face when working with children from a very young age and offers guidance for best practice.

Lambert, M. (2008) 'Devil in the detail: using a pupil questionnaire survey in an evaluation of out-of-school classes for gifted and talented children', *Education 3–13*, 36(1), 69–78.
My article explores issues of ethics, design, bias and interpretation in relation to the use of questionnaires.

Lewis, A. and Lindsay G. (eds) (2000) *Researching Children's Perspectives.* Buckingham: Open University Press.
Among the books on children's participation in research, this is one of the most interesting. The authors discuss a range of issues, including ethics, vulnerable groups, children's rights and even children's capacity to carry out their own investigations.

10 Carrying out your investigation

What will you learn from this chapter?

In this chapter, we discuss how you can choose and arrange access to a centre, school, college or other educational setting in order to carry out your investigation. We also consider how you should behave as a researcher, from your first contact to the collection of data and completion of your work.

Choosing your venue

Choosing a suitable venue is an important aspect of your project. You need somewhere which is suitable for your chosen topic and where you can reach appropriate participants. Ideally, it is also good to have a venue where your presence as a researcher is actively welcomed, possibly because of the potential benefits of your work for the development of its practice.

Using contacts

Previous acquaintance or personal contact with staff can facilitate access, so you will probably think first of these possibilities:

- a place where you work or have worked, as a member of staff, on student placement or as a volunteer
- a centre, school or college that your own child or a close relative attends
- where you yourself were educated
- another educational setting where staff know you and you know them.

If you do have prior acquaintance of this kind, tell your contact about your project, get an indication if doing your investigation there might be possible, and be prepared to request access formally in writing from the head or manager of that venue. Even if you are known at the setting, a concise, informative letter of this kind will help to establish your new role as a researcher. Here is a suggested structure for this:

1   In the first paragraph, say who you are and the nature of your course of study.
2   In the second paragraph, give the topic of your research, indicate your wish to carry it out at this venue and give a reason for this request.
3   In the third paragraph, give an indication of what your research will involve. Indicate briefly how you will respect the anonymity of participants and confidentiality of data.
4   In the final paragraph, indicate your readiness to discuss your research further at a face-to-face meeting.
5   Finally, give your full contact details so that the venue can contact you about your request.

Here are some extra tips:

- **Tone:** Be polite but assured in your writing.
- **Length and accuracy:** Your letter should be less than one full page. It *must* be fully accurate – jump ahead to Chapter 12 to see what common mistakes to avoid.
- **Your research brief:** Attach to the letter the research brief you drew up at the end of Chapter 9. Refer to it in the letter itself: 'The attached research brief gives more information about my project'.
- **Using your contact:** Your contact may allow you to mention them in your letter. For example: 'I have already discussed my project informally with your assistant headteacher, and she has suggested that I write to you with this request'.
- **Leaving yourself a follow-up option:** Do not simply ask the venue to contact you in response to your letter – you will be left in limbo if they do not do so. Leave open the option of telephoning again in a few days' time to follow up your request.
- **Keeping a copy:** Keep a copy of your letter to include as an appendix in your written project.

There can, however, be disadvantages with this kind of arrangement. For instance, if participants already know you as a colleague and friend, they may find it hard to see you in your new role of objective researcher, and this may influence the way they respond to your research. It may be awkward for you to adopt and maintain a neutral stance while collecting data, or to offer critical comment as a result of your investigation. If your venue is your current place of work, check what Blaxter et al. (2010: 48) have to say about the particular problems you may face.

Approaching 'cold'…

So even if you have contacts at a potential venue, you might consider approaching a different venue 'cold', even though it is more difficult to arrange access when no one knows who you are. You will have to do this anyway if you do not have personal contacts with a venue at which your topic could be investigated. In this case, sending a letter like the one described above will be an important way of making your request, but here are some extra steps to take before you do this:

1 Using its website and online inspection reports, find out as much as you can about the venue: the nature of the establishment, the names of senior staff, the nature of its work, especially aspects of its practice it wishes currently to strengthen or develop.

2 Telephone the venue and ask to speak to a relevant senior staff member. Explain briefly the reason for your call.

3 You may not get any further than the person who answers the phone. This person may wish to take your message and pass it on, or ask you to put your request in writing. In this case, start your letter by saying that you have already telephoned: 'I refer to my recent telephone call about my request to carry out research at your school. Thank you for inviting me to send you more details about this'.

4 Your aim, as a result of either your call or your letter, should be to arrange an opportunity to discuss your research with a senior member of staff.

 Activity 10.1   Debbie's inappropriate letter

Debbie has written a letter to her potential research venue in rather a rush, to put it mildly. Help her to improve it (my suggestions are in Appendix II).

Birmingham
Tuesday

Deputy Principal
Nonsuch College

Dear Bill,

Hi! I am a student and want to do my project at your college. I want to do it there because it is easy for me to get there on the bus. I want to tork to tutors and kids about my project. I will come to tell you more about it next Tuesday at 9.00.

Love from Debs xx
P.S. My project is about Art and Design

 **Key Points**

> If at first you don't succeed … do not be too discouraged. If a venue refuses your request, try to find out the reasons why, then start your process again with another venue, or discuss options with your project tutor.

Your first appointment

Let us assume that things have gone well. You have arranged a formal appointment with a senior member of staff at an appropriate research venue to discuss your intentions. You will wish to make a good impression at this meeting – here are some suggestions on how to prepare:

- Make sure the person you are due to talk to has a copy of your research brief in advance. Take extra copies to the meeting for other members of staff.

- Be prepared at the meeting to explain and discuss your research, justify your choice of topic and venue, and explain how you will carry out your investigation. Be prepared also to consider adaptations and refinements to your plans in response to issues raised.

- Be ready to offer something in return: for instance, a written summary when your research is complete, or a presentation at a staff meeting (we discuss such opportunities in Chapter 12). Many venues will value this contribution to their developmental work.

- Take your diary so you can arrange follow-up meetings if appropriate.

Arranging data collection

If your meeting goes well, you can start preparing for your data collection. For this you will need to:

- explain your research to those who you wish to involve (your research brief will again be useful here)

- seek 'informed consent' from potential participants – you will need to decide if you need active or presumed consent (see Chapter 9) and formulate your requests accordingly

- plan a suitable timetable for your data collection.

Lakshmi plans her data collection

Lakshmi has had her first meeting about her project on the place of science in the curriculum with the school where she would like to do her research (she did a placement there earlier in her course). The meeting went well – the assistant headteacher with whom she spoke was satisfied that Lakshmi had planned her investigation well and indicated that she would be able to do it at the school. Lakshmi arranged to talk at a staff meeting the following week – there she will explain her research again and indicate her wish, with agreement, to interview selected staff. The assistant headteacher also said that she could talk to students the following week, and all being well they would complete her questionnaire (unless they wished not to) during science lessons shortly after. Lakshmi will also write to parents about her research – she feels (and the school agrees) that it is sufficient to inform them about the questionnaire their children will be completing, and simply to invite those with queries or concerns to get in touch via the school office.

Your conduct as a researcher 'in the field'

You have now reached a very significant point in your project. Reading and analysing books, designing research questions, choosing methods – all are vital, but collecting data in the field is what research is all about and is the basis of your project's contribution to knowledge and understanding. So use your energies to make a success of all the plans you have made and the exciting stage you have reached.

We continue this chapter, therefore, with a careful look at your behaviour as an active researcher in educational settings. I make no apologies for going through this, as your conduct is so important, both for your credibility and for the reputation of the institution which as a student you represent.

If you are training to be a teacher, or are a teacher already, you already have codes of professional practice with which you will be familiar – these are useful for doing research too. For instance, in England there is the Code of Professional Values and Practice for Teachers; in Scotland the Code of Professionalism and Conduct (COPAC); whilst the USA has a code produced by the Association of American Educators. To find your relevant code, search online for 'Code of practice for teachers in ...' followed by the relevant country or American state. In addition, here is my more specific advice about how to behave whilst doing your research.

Arrival

- **Punctuality:** Arrive a few minutes earlier than arranged, but not too early. Be courteous and patient, especially if you arrive at a busy time such as the start of a day. If you are unavoidably late, get a message to the venue to explain this and give your expected time of arrival.
- **Procedures:** Be prepared to follow procedures on arrival, for instance signing the visitors' book, wearing a visitors' badge, reading fire procedures. Take photo ID with you, for example your student card – you may be asked to show it.
- **Criminal records check:** In many countries, those who work with children and young people have a criminal records check. If this applies to you, take your certificate with you as well – some establishments may also wish to see this. Some may even require that you undergo a new and separate check before doing your research (see Chapter 2).

Appearance and behaviour

- **Dress:** Practice varies, but for your first visit err on the more formal side. This means no jeans, trainers (unless you are observing sport or physical education), skimpy clothing or excessive jewellery. I have known schools object to unusually coloured hair, uncovered tattoos and men without ties.
- **Refreshments:** Find out what is acceptable, for instance where you can eat a packed lunch or have a hot drink. Be prepared to pay for any meal or drinks provided by your venue. Never chew gum.
- **Use of resources:** Always ask if you can photocopy and offer to pay.
- **Personal property:** Leave valuables at home wherever possible and keep personal property secure.
- **Mobile phones:** Many venues, in particular those with young children, have strict rules about mobile phones. Some may require you to hand yours in at reception. If you must take one, keep it switched off and hidden. If you wish to make or take a call, ask where this is best done. You should *never* take photographs or film, with a phone or camera, unless you have clear and specific permission to do so (see Chapters 8 and 9).

Attendance

- **Absence**: If you find you cannot attend an arranged visit, get a phone message to your research venue as soon as possible. Ask that this message gets to relevant staff, for example those you intended to observe or interview that day. Contact the venue again once you are ready to restart your work.

- **Illness**: If you are ill, postpone your visit until you are sure you will not pass your infection on to others.

- **Helping out**: As staff get to know you well, you may be asked to do things not connected with your research, for instance provide extra adult supervision on an educational trip or even cover an unexpected staff absence. It can be difficult to know what to do in these situations. You may feel obliged to help or you may feel that this is not your role and that once accepted, requests could get out of hand. My advice here is to seek a balance. Help if you can and if the request seems reasonable. If you cannot, or if it seems too onerous or inappropriate, explain your difficulty to a relevant member of staff, acting professionally throughout. You may feel more able to offer help, for instance with a trip, once your research is completed.

Collecting data

- **Preparation**: Be well prepared for data-collection events. Make time beforehand to get together your materials and to remind yourself of what you have arranged to do, the names of your participants and what you wish to achieve.

- **Research instruments**: A first task will be to 'pilot' your research instruments (see Chapter 9), then to adjust and improve them as a result of what you learn, ready for your real collection of data.

- **Questionnaires**: Check you have enough copies and take spare pens too. You want this process to go briskly and smoothly.

- **Interviews**: Check your voice recorder is working (if you have consented to use it) and take spare batteries; or check you are ready to take written notes. Some researchers like to give out their main questions in advance, so that interviewees can consider how they will respond.

- **Observation**: At the start of your observation, make notes about its context: the venue, number of students, number and nature of staff, theme of the lesson. There is a box in the observation framework in Project Sheet 11 (Appendix I) for this. While observing as a non-participant (see Chapter 7), try not to disturb normal activity. If a child seeks your attention or help, either direct the child in silent but friendly fashion back towards the lesson, or give brief, cautious help if normal sources of assistance are not available.

- **Notes:** Be ready to explain to your participants what kind of notes you are taking. Do not leave your notes lying around for others to find.
- **Thank you:** Of course, always thank those involved for their contributions.

Relationships with students

- **Respect:** Show the same level of respect to children and students as you do to adults.
- **Distance:** Keep a distance – both physically and socially – between yourself and children or students. Be friendly by all means, but do not try to get acquainted more closely than is necessary for you to do your research.
- **Role model:** Even if your contact is relatively brief, you should be a 'positive role model'. Behave considerately and show your willingness to work hard.
- **School rules:** Get to know your venue's rules – do not tempt children or students to break these. If some seem to take advantage of the fact that you are not a member of staff, seek advice about what to do.
- **Language:** Bad language is disrespectful to others. Never use bad language yourself or allow it in others. If it occurs in your interviews or group discussions, ask that such language is not used. If it continues, then end the discussion early.
- **Safety:** As an adult, you have responsibilities, as do others, to protect the safety of children and students. Never put them (or other adults) in situations where they are at risk.
- **Physical contact:** Make it a general rule not to have any physical contact with children or students. There may be rare exceptions, for instance comforting a distressed child. In these circumstances:
  - use only the physical contact which is required, such as an arm around the shoulder
  - do so openly, not hiding what you are doing
  - end the physical contact as soon as it is reasonable to do so
  - hand the episode over to a member of staff as soon as you can
  - never ever strike, pull or push a student or child. The very least that will happen is that you will be asked to leave and your research at that venue will cease. You can find further advice on physical contact at government websites relevant to your own country.
- **Meetings:** Never ask children or students to meet you away from the venue. If as part of your research you wish to meet them at their home, then this must be arranged through the venue and the parents or carers, and you must ensure that parents or carers are present when you visit.

Relationships with staff

- **Respect:** Staff includes many people: teachers, assistants, lunchtime supervisors, caretaker and cleaning personnel, secretaries, and so on. Treat them all with respect and professional friendliness. Also respect the authority of the headteacher, principal or other senior staff, and of teachers and others in any classes you observe – do not undermine their work.

- **Greetings:** Be friendly and communicative – greet staff on arrival, learn names and cooperate with what is going on, without overstepping your researcher role.

- **Explanations:** Always be ready once again to introduce yourself and explain your research. Everyone involved (staff and students) has a right to know who you are and what you are doing.

- **Conversations:** Never engage in gossip, however – stay uninvolved or move away if you hear this going on. Never make derogatory comments to one member of staff about another.

- **Social media:** Never write about your venue or anyone you meet there on social media such as Facebook or Twitter – doing so is highly disrespectful. Even apparently positive comments can be misinterpreted or cause offence. My advice also is not to have as a friend on such media anyone connected with your venue. It is always wholly inappropriate to have children or students as friends on such media.

- **Balance:** Be understanding of the pressures which staff work under. Strike a balance between getting your research done and recognizing the wider responsibilities of staff at your venue.

Relationships with parents

- **Respect:** Show respect for the home life of children and students with whom you have contact. It is not your role to judge.

- **Work through school:** If you wish for contact with parents or carers, arrange this in cooperation with your research venue. Make use of normal events (for example, a weekly parents' coffee morning) to get to know them, explain your research and even to do your data collection.

How to leave

- **Next visit:** Make sure everyone is clear about the arrangements for your next visit.

- **Departure:** Sign out at reception. Remember a final thank you to reception staff, perhaps with a reminder of when you expect to be at the venue again.

And finally...

- **Back up your data:** As soon as you can, back up any data you have collected and transcribed electronically. If lost, and you have no copy, you could find yourself collecting data all over again...
- **Inform your tutor:** Keep your tutor informed of how you get on. At the end of your data collection, a face-to-face tutorial may be useful, to discuss your experiences and how you intend to analyse the data you have collected. This is the next important stage of your project – we focus on it in the following chapter.

Further reading 📖

Phinn, G. (1999) *The Other Side of the Dale*. London: Penguin.
Gervase Phinn's humorous accounts (this and other collections) of a school inspector's experiences in the north of England may seem an odd recommendation. However, Mr Phinn's polite but perceptive responses to events which variously amuse, confuse or concern him (and to those which warm his heart) may help shape your own behaviour in educational contexts – and give you some very entertaining reading along the way.

SECTION THREE

Analysing and Writing Up

11 Analysing data and producing your findings

What will you learn from this chapter?

The reason for doing research is to produce interesting and valuable findings, drawn from collected data and which answer pre-determined research questions. This chapter looks at some processes of analysis which make this possible, and which allow you to produce conclusions and recommendations to inform professional practice and continuing research.

Analysis

We first defined the term 'analysis' in Chapter 6, when discussing how to put together your literature review. The same basic principles of 'breaking down' and 'making connections' apply here too, only this time in relation to the data you have gathered. We will examine some of the processes involved in this chapter in relation to quantitative, then to qualitative data.

First, however, you should be aware of your own responsibilities in this process in relation to validity, reliability and ethics. When analysing data, you should try as best you can to reflect honestly what people have written or said, or what you have observed. You should maintain a balanced, professional approach when presenting what you have discovered and ensure that any judgements arise from your data, not from prior beliefs or opinions of your own.

Charlotte considers the ethics of her data analysis

Charlotte has investigated the use of peer tutoring amongst students at the school where she works. Her findings are rather uncomplimentary about these arrangements, and she worries about how her colleagues will react to her conclusions. She resolves to focus on her data, analysing them as objectively and carefully as she can, and when the time comes, to write them up in a professional manner, respecting the anonymity of those who contributed. She decides that the more objective her approach, the more constructive will be the reaction when she shares her findings with the school.

Analysing quantitative data

We look first at some basic procedures for analysing quantitative data. These data involve numbers and come from sources such as these:

- counting factual data, for instance: *How many female students completed the questionnaire? How many male students?*
- closed questions in questionnaires or interviews, for instance: *How many years have you taught at this school? Where would you grade this facility on a five-point scale?*
- counting events during observation, for instance: *How many times did the teacher praise the children for good behaviour?*
- counting elements in qualitative data, for instance: *How many times did interviewees mention a specific teaching technique?*
- results of tests, examinations or other assessments
- other sources of statistics, for example government reports, institutional data.

Items such as these result in 'variables', characteristics of data (for instance, gender, age, the ethnicity of sampled participants, or their experiences, achievements or opinions), which we are interested in investigating further.

Processes

Analysing quantitative data involves three basic processes:

1 **Counting** reveals the frequency with which something happens, for example: *How many students achieved the top grade in their examination?* In research language, this is called 'frequency distribution'.

2 **Separating out** shows the frequency with which something applies to different groups. For instance: *How many male students achieved top grades? How many female students? How many from Class A achieved top grades? How many from Class B?* This process is called 'cross-tabulation'.

3 **Comparing** helps you find possible patterns or 'relationships' between sets of data. For instance: *Female students in Class B were most likely to achieve a top grade. Male students in Class A were least likely to get a top grade.* This is called 'correlation'.

 Hannah analyses quantitative data

Hannah and Andrew are co-researchers investigating students' use of computers. They divide the analysis of quantitative data between them. Hannah looks first at responses given to a closed question which asked respondents to consider the statement: 'I get bored using computers in school'. She counts the responses given and records them as shown in Figure 11.1.

Strongly agree	Partially agree	Neutral	Partially disagree	Strongly disagree	No response
9	20	7	10	3	1

n = 50

Figure 11.1 Hannah counts her quantitative data

The questionnaire also asked for the gender of respondents. Hannah uses this additional information to separate out the data, as shown in Figure 11.2.

	Strongly agree	Partially agree	Neutral	Partially disagree	Strongly disagree	No response
Boys (n = 24)	2	7	6	8	0	1
Girls (n = 26)	7	13	1	2	3	0
Total	9	20	7	10	3	1

Figure 11.2 Hannah separates out her quantitative data

(Continued)

(Continued)

> She can now make comparisons between the variables she has established. Her data indicate that slightly more girls than boys responded to the question and that they were more willing to state a firm opinion. Boys generally agreed less with the statement than girls, but only girls disagreed with it completely. With appropriate data, Hannah could use similar processes to compare other variables, for instance responses of older and younger students, or the views amongst different ethnic groups, or of students with different examination grades.

Note these features of Hannah's presentation of data:

- **'n =':** 'n' denotes the number of respondents whose data are presented. Hannah's charts show data from 50 respondents overall; 24 are from boys and 26 from girls.

- **Missing data:** One male respondent has not answered this question, perhaps by mistake, perhaps because he did not wish to do so. Hannah has felt it useful to include this in her table. A large amount of missing data could indicate a problem with a question or with the questionnaire as a whole.

- **Percentages:** In the case study, Hannah cited raw numbers, not percentages. This is because her sample is relatively small. If she had more responses, for instance over 100, using percentages instead might improve clarity.

 ## Activity 11.1 Andrew's analysis of quantitative data

The questionnaire also asked respondents to put in order of importance from 1 to 5 why they use a computer at home (1 indicated the most important reason, 5 the least). Andrew sets out responses for the first five respondents, as shown in Figure 11.3.

Respondent (n = 5)	A.Writing notes	B.Searching Internet	C. Social networking	D. Email etc.	E. Looking at college intranet
A	4	1	3	2	5
B	4	1	5	2	3
C	4	1	2	3	5

D	3	5	1	2	4
E	4	1	5	2	3
Total	19	9	16	11	20

Figure 11.3   Andrew's quantitative data

> Examine Andrew's sets of data. What do they indicate so far about the popularity of different kinds of computer usage? With more data, how might Andrew identify responses of different groups? What kind of data would he need to have collected to do this? Some answers are in Appendix II.

Hannah and Andrew are examining their initial information mentally or with a calculator. With further data from more respondents, they could find out more in this way. For instance, they could add up how many respondents were aged under 18 and how many were 18 or older; how many of the younger students agreed with a statement and how many older ones agreed with it too (more 'counting' and 'separating'). They could notice possible patterns amongst variables, for instance, that younger students seem more likely to look at the college intranet than older ones, or that younger students from one ethnic background appear to enjoy social networking more than older students from other backgrounds (more 'comparing'). Note, however, that doing such analysis depends on them having collected sufficient relevant data in the first place: without data there can be no analysis.

Concepts

Hannah and Andrew are using some basic mathematics and cautious common sense to describe their quantitative data. As a beginner researcher, you may not wish to do more than this. However, if you want more precise analysis, there are some important concepts to take on board.

First of all, there is not one type of quantitative data but several. For instance:

- **Nominal data** are numbers which you assign to unranked categories. For instance, you assign the label '1' to male students; '2' to female students. You could do the same with staff: teachers (1) and non-teachers (2), or teachers of science (1), English (2) and mathematics (3). Nominal data are helpful when entering data into computer software (see below).

- **Ordinal data** are the kind of data which Hannah was dealing with above. Again, these data stand for categories, but the categories are ranked in an order – strongly disagree through to strongly agree, for instance. However, the categories are essentially (in research terms at least) rather imprecise.
- **Interval data** are ranked in order too, but the categories and the distance between them are more precisely defined. For instance, the first day of each year (1 January 2005, 1 January 2006, etc.) is interval data – the categories are precise and the differences between them are the same (apart from leap years).

Much statistical analysis is concerned with how data relate to a middle point or average of some kind. There are specific concepts which help researchers to do this. For instance:

- The **mean** is the average, so if students' examination marks are 24, 28, 34 and 34, the mean is 30.
- The **median** is the middle category point in a set of data. In these examination data, the median figure is half way between 24 and 34, which is 29.
- The **mode** is the most common response, so for those same data it is 34. Mean, median and mode are all ways of finding typical or average values in sets of data, known as **central tendency**. Different types of data require different measures of central tendency for their analysis.
- **Range** is the distance between the two extremes of data. In this example, the extremes are 24 and 34, so the range is the difference: 10. Range is a measure of the 'spread' of the data.

Being aware of these measures allows researchers to look at how items of data, known as 'values', are placed. For instance:

- Values may be placed fairly symmetrically on each side of the mean, with most placed close to it. If the examination marks of five other students were 21, 27, 28, 30 and 34, their distribution is of this kind – the mean mark is 28 and there is a reasonable balance of values either side of this.
- However, data could diverge or be 'skewed' from the mean. If the marks are 24, 26, 26, 28 and 36, the mean is still 28 but most values are below this. If the marks are 18, 25, 29, 33 and 35, the mean is still 28 but most values are above the mean.
- These features (and others) – more meaningful when applied to larger sets of data – relate to what is known as **standard deviation**: 'a measure of the extent to which values in a distribution cluster about the mean' (Muijs, 2011: 93). Measuring this is the basis for much analysis of quantitative data.

Computer software

Basit (2010: 169) shows how to work out measures of standard deviation with a calculator. However, for ease of analysis and with more extensive or complex data, most researchers turn to specialist data-processing computer software, such as these:

- **Excel**: With Excel you can enter data in cells, give each cell a reference (A1; B2) and set up automatic calculations, for example: Cell C3 = C1+ C2. Thomas (2009: 212–225) describes its use for a range of analytical tasks.

- **IBM SPSS (Statistical Package for the Social Sciences)**: This is a more specialist programme, with versions for Windows and for Mac (www.spss.com). With preparation it is nevertheless very accessible, even for beginners. Your university or college probably holds a licence for it. Muijs (2011) provides a clear, step-by-step guide to its use.

Computer software can handle large amounts of information quickly (as long as you enter the data first, of course), and makes possible more complicated calculations. These can involve potential predictions about relationships between variables. For example, most respondents agree with a statement, but how confident can you be that most other people who did not take part in your investigation would agree with it likewise?

An important element of this is the calculation of **statistical significance**. This indicates whether a relationship between variables in the data (such as older students apparently using the college intranet less than younger ones) is likely to have occurred in your data by chance, or because that relationship really does exist or occurs more widely. Or as Muijs (2011: 98) explains it, using terms we defined in Chapter 7, there is 'low probability of [it] occurring in the sample, if there was no relationship in the population'. Predictive analysis of this kind helps researchers to assess the extent to which findings can be generalized beyond the participant group – we consider this notion of 'generalizability' further in the next chapter.

As you can tell, analysing quantitative data involves the use of some unfamiliar terminology and particular techniques. This puts many researchers, especially beginners, off this kind of approach. However, it can add value to an investigation, and some techniques – counting, separating, describing patterns and possible relationships – are ones which you (like Hannah and Andrew) can do fairly easily, as long as you are cautious about what you find. Even measures of statistical significance are reasonably straightforward – with further reading, a careful approach and reasonable amounts of suitable quantitative data to work with, you could even take this on too.

Finally, there is another purpose of quantitative data analysis: to find out how one variable may or may not influence another – cause and effect. You will recall our first cautionary discussion of this back in Chapter 4. Take note, therefore, of Muijs' (2011: 19–29) interesting discussion on this issue; also of Thomas' (2009: 220) advice: 'When we look for relationships between variables we have to be very wary about imputing reasons for any relationships we discover'. In a beginner's project, unless you have strong understanding of techniques for collecting and analysing quantitative data, understanding too of how to use computer software for this, it is unlikely that you will be in a position to look for causality in this way.

Analysing qualitative data

Qualitative data, involving words and phrases, are most likely to come from:

- answers to open questions in questionnaires
- interview transcripts
- notes taken during observation
- analysis of documents relating to your topic.

In their raw state, your data are probably organized in relation to their sources: everything Respondent A has said is together; everything Respondent B has said, and so on. Analysis means reorganizing these data, so that they are grouped around particular themes and ideas instead. The process involves scribbling and annotation, so a set of coloured or highlighter pens, or the equivalent toolbar on your computer, is useful for this.

First steps

First, collect your qualitative data together, make a copy and use this copy for your analysis. Number the lines or sections of your transcript, so you can refer to them easily. Make three columns: in the first put the text you are analysing, the second is for your analysis, the third for extra thoughts and ideas. Now follow this process:

1 **Read your data closely**: or, with a voice recording, listen to it several times. The more familiar you are with your data, the better your analysis will be.
2 **Identify common themes**: What main themes are evident? Highlight where these themes occur and give a label (a word or abbreviation) to each theme in your notes. The 'find' facility on your computer (Ctrl + F on Microsoft; cmd + F on Apple) may help you with this.

3 **Find perspectives**: Note also what your respondents say about these themes – their 'perspective', or with observation, how participants have behaved or reacted in relation to these themes. Highlight and label these too.

4 **Identify representative quotations or events**: Highlight small items of data (a phrase or sentence, or an item of observation) which illustrate a particular theme, perspective or behaviour.

5 **Keep thinking**: Use your third column to jot down any ideas that occur to you as you do this analysis.

 ## Activity 11.2   Nick's analysis

Nick has voice-recorded, then transcribed, an interview with children about how they view the difficulty of school work. Figure 11.4 is his first attempt at analysis. Examine it and decide: What key themes has he identified so far? What perspectives has he noticed? What extra thoughts has he had about his data? You can see Nick's own summary in a case study later in this chapter.

	Time (mins)	Speaker	Text	Analysis	Notes
1	000	Nick	In your view, what does 'difficult' mean?		
2		Jamal	Difficult is it's hard.		
3		Jordan	When something is new, you haven't done it before.	Newness	
4		Jalene	It's like it's just out of reach from your ability to do it.	Not within capabilities	
5	0.20	Jake	Like when Miss asks a question and I don't understand it.	Not understanding	Aspect of 'not within capabilities'?
6		Jamal	And we have to ask her to explain what she means.	Need for help	
7		Jordan	And when she uses strange words that I can't understand.	Terminology	
8		Jake	New words.	Newness	Relates to 'not understanding' above
9		Jalene	You have to think quickly.	Pace	

(Continued)

(Continued)

10		Jordan	It makes my head ache.	Interesting, but what exactly did Jordan mean by this?
11	1.00	Jamal	I like thinking. It's good.	Also interesting ...

Figure 11.4   Nick's analysis of qualitative data

Coding

The process above is often called 'coding': 'Coding is simply a process of classifying chunks of your interview data and observations into key themes or headlines' (Roberts-Holmes, 2011: 186–187). Nick above uses labels such as 'newness' and 'pace' for this, but you may find you can also devise a real code – abbreviations or coloured highlighting – to speed up your analysis. It is important to use the same coding system across all of your qualitative data, no matter where it has come from (for instance, Nick could also try to identify these features, using the same terms, in his observation records). As we will see, this will help you greatly to 'integrate' your data.

Coding like this may seem fairly straightforward, but it can be tricky. One reason is that it is not always easy to interpret or categorize what respondents, especially children, say, write or do (see, for example, Nick's note about Jordan's 'headache' response). You may have to make difficult decisions when interpreting the data you have collected. Here are some further examples of data from Nick's interviews and other methods, and the interpretation difficulties arising from them:

- *I enjoy being able to do difficult things.* Does 'being able' mean having the capability to do difficult things, or being allowed to do them – or both?
- *I enjoy being able to get help and doing it myself.* There seem to be two contradictory perspectives in this single response.
- *The staff say really hard words – when I ask them what it means, they make it even more difficult.* This is an important response, but working out how to code it will not be easy.
- *Student falls asleep in class.* Does this observation mean that the student was bored, or tired out, or both?
- *This is easy!* Was the student here being critical or complimentary?

- *Activities should provide a combination of challenge and fun.* Does this policy statement mean that each activity should be both difficult and enjoyable, or that there should be different activities, some challenging, others just 'fun'?

For this reason (and other reasons), it is unreasonable to expect analysis of qualitative data to lead to firm conclusions and reach a single 'truth'. Rather, it produces meaning from your interpretation of your data. This meaning may be strong and persuasive, but nevertheless another researcher might have done it differently, identified other themes and perspectives, presumed different meanings. This is why we associate qualitative data with an 'interpretivist' paradigm (see Chapter 1).

Reorganizing analysed data

You now have coded data. Your next step is to reorganize these according to the codes, like this:

1 **Group your data**: Make a list of the themes and perspectives you have identified. Then collect all the data from all your methods relating to each theme and each perspective on that theme. For example, if a common theme in your data is 'student achievement', draw together all data that you have collected from all your methods about this theme. If one perspective on that theme is about the importance of good teaching, identify all the data within the group that give that perspective. If another perspective is about the role of parental expectation, bring those data together too (note how this grouping process is rather similar to how you handled material in your literature review in Chapter 6). We call this 'integrating' your data.

2 **Examine data**: Now look at what you have got. You will see how a particular theme or perspective has a range of evidence relating to it. You may be able to assess the strength and complexity of these ideas too: one with a substantial supporting data will seem more persuasive than one with little to back it up.

3 **Compare themes and perspectives**: Now examine how these various themes and perspectives relate to each other. Are themes completely separate, or are there links between them? Do different perspectives show agreement or disagreement? Do they reflect different interests, emphases or priorities? Again, this process is similar to the process of agreement and contrast which you tackled in your literature review, except that now you are applying it to your collected data.

4 **Dig deep**: Keep scrutinizing your analysed data. As well as links, similarities and differences, look for contradictions, uncertainties, tensions, dilemmas. Find complexity in ideas and how they relate to

each other. This is often called 'interrogating your data', gaining as much understanding as you can from the data you have collected (my term is again 'digging deep'). The more thoroughly you do this, the more valuable your research.

 Nick interrogates his data about 'difficult' work

We left Nick exploring themes and perspectives in his interview data. After more analysis of this kind, with data from teachers as well as children, he records his thoughts in his research log:

My data from children have produced a range of perspectives about the notion of 'difficulty'. Some respondents see a sense of novelty about difficult work (I labelled this 'newness'), often associated with new words ('terminology') or with the speed of tasks ('pace'). Some children said they did not like difficult work, but others were more positive – they saw it as motivating, just as most teachers said it should be in my other data. My classroom observations threw up this contradiction too: children often complained that something was difficult, but when the work was too easy they got bored and complained about that too! Getting the level and type of difficulty just right may be a very important aspect of successful teaching.

Other methods of analysis

The approach above is useful for many types of data. However, there are many others. Here are some you might find appropriate:

- **Discourse analysis:** With this approach, you analyse conversations in very close detail: vocabulary, tone of voice, how participants initiate or respond to dialogue. You 'unpack the text' (Denscombe, 2010: 287), looking for clues about participants' assumptions or motivations. For instance, a speaker's choice of words may give indications of their attitude towards gender equality. You need exact transcriptions of conversations to adopt this approach.
- **Sociograms:** These diagrams are most commonly used to map relationships between people: who talks to whom, who is friends with whom. They could, for instance, help you understand from whom teachers seek guidance to strengthen their practice. Thomas (2009: 208–210) describes this approach.

- **'Thick description'**: When observing you may wish to deduce reasons for the behaviour you see: not just what is happening but why. This involves close scrutiny both of the behaviour itself and of the context in which it takes place, and is sometimes known as 'thick description'. This approach may be valuable but can be very difficult to do – see Chapter 1 of Geertz (2000), republished from 1973, for a vivid account of the detail which might be involved.

Specialist software

Beginner researchers will normally analyse qualitative data 'by hand' or using simple word-processing computer software. However, there is also specialist computer software for this task, for instance NVivo (pronounced 'en-vee-voe' – see Bazeley, 2007) and ATLAS.ti (see Friese, 2011). These programmes are useful where there are substantial qualitative data which require detailed and sophisticated analysis (you will also need access to a licence to use them). However, learning to use such software effectively takes quite a long time – my advice for beginners is to stick to more straightforward methods.

Producing your findings

You have now analysed data in various forms: numbers, themes, perspectives on those themes, and started to see relationships or links between them. You now need to derive some greater meaning from all of this. The result will be your 'findings' – what you have discovered as a result of your research. These findings must be credible: your reader must be able to share your belief that they reflect what analysis of your data has revealed. I suggest four stages for this process:

1 Determine your findings.
2 Discuss your findings.
3 Draw up conclusions.
4 Produce recommendations.

1. Determine your findings

You do this by relating the outcomes of your analysis to the research questions you wish to answer. A useful first step is simply to list your research questions, each on a separate page. Note down beneath each question any analysis outcome which relates to and helps to answer that question. Examine the overall picture produced and summarize what you have found out.

Jude uses integrated data to produce a finding about curriculum development training

Jude has a research question about obstacles to making changes in a college curriculum. Three themes in her data help her to answer this question. The first is the perspective that lecturers' lack of training on curriculum development is the biggest obstacle – this perspective was expressed in interviews with senior staff. The second is the view that lack of time for such training is the biggest obstacle – this was evident in quantitative data from questionnaires and in qualitative data from interviews. Jude's third theme, evident in her analysis of college documents and some interview transcripts, is that while training is an aim, few training opportunities are taken up. Her first finding, drawn from all these sets of data, is that while training is needed and the wish for training is strong, practical issues, in particular a lack of time, mean that the college is not meeting its aspirations in this area. This finding helps to answer Jude's research question about obstacles to change.

If you have collected sufficient, relevant data and analysed these data closely, you should be able to produce several findings of this kind against each of your research questions. For instance, Jude may find she can identify further obstacles, such as a lack of appropriate facilities and funding constraints. If you cannot identify further findings, then examine your data again: 'dig deep'. If this fails too, you may have found a weakness in your research: insufficient data to produce relevant findings. Keep a note of this difficulty – you may need to discuss it when you consider in the recommendations section of your project how your investigation might be extended or improved (see section 4 below).

2. Discuss your findings

You should now have findings against each of your research questions. The next stage is to 'discuss' them, in your head, by scribbling your thoughts down as notes, and ultimately as formal discussion in your written project. Here are some questions you can ask yourself in order to do this:

- What is interesting about your findings?
- What is unclear or uncertain about them?

- How do different findings relate to each other? Are they consistent? Are there tensions or contradictions between them?
- How important do your findings appear to be?
- To what extent do they provide answers to your research questions? What still remains to be discovered?
- How do your findings relate to the ideas you examined in your literature review?

This last point is important. As you analyse your data and produce your findings, you will be reminded of what you read and wrote about when doing your literature review (Chapter 6). Jude, for instance, may find that the obstacles to curriculum development identified in her data match perspectives expressed in books and journal articles she examined earlier. She could also find, of course, that her findings contradicted ideas in the literature, or raised issues not found there at all – this might make her research particularly interesting. As you scrutinize your findings, take note of their relationship to the literature you examined – this will be an important aspect in your discussion of findings when you write up your project (see Chapter 12).

3. Draw up conclusions

Determining and discussing findings takes time; drawing conclusions should be a simpler (but still very important) process. For conclusions, summarize your main findings in clear and concise form – in your written project, you may even present them as a list. If you have organized your themed data well against your research questions, you should be able to do this fairly easily. Do these checks at the same time:

- Do your summarized findings clearly answer each of your research questions? As far as possible they should.
- Do they clearly relate to the data you collected (or have you 'made things up', without data evidence for them)? Conclusions should, of course, clearly emerge from your analysis of collected data.

4. Produce recommendations

The final task is to work out the recommendations which arise from your research – what useful advice you can provide to others as a result of your investigation. First, we must consider two relevant concepts: 'generalizability' and 'relatability'.

Generalizability means the extent to which your findings apply, not just to the people who took part in your investigation or the setting where you carried it out, but to other people or other settings also. With small-scale exploratory research, it is rare for findings to be generalizable in this way. A more relevant concept for your research is **relatability**. This means that other people and settings, especially those similar to your participants and research venue, may well be able to learn and gain benefit from what you have found out. There are sufficient similarities between your participants and those who did not participate, or between your research venue and other situations, to inform practice beyond the context of your investigation. When you produce recommendations, work on the basis that your findings may be 'relatable' to other people or settings, but that it is unlikely they will be 'generalizable'.

 My science investigation

I have investigated students' views on how combustion of materials should be taught in a secondary school. I think my findings must show how students elsewhere view teaching of this topic also. However, my tutor points out that just because I found these views in one school does not mean that they are the same amongst students elsewhere as well. The findings of my research are not 'generalizable'. However, other similar secondary schools will be interested in what I discovered and my findings could inform their practice. Policy makers too may feel that my research can inform their thinking. My findings may therefore be 'relatable' to these other contexts.

Bearing this in mind, start to work out what your recommendations should be. They can cover two main areas – educational recommendations and recommendations for research.

Recommendations for education: For these, ask yourself: 'How do my conclusions inform development of educational thinking and practice:

- at my research venue?
- in similar educational settings?
- at a local and national policy level?
- in relation to my own practice and development?'

Recommendations for research: For these, ask yourself:

- How could the research which I carried out be improved or extended?

- What further research should be carried out, by myself or by others, to find out more about the topic or to resolve issues raised by my investigation?

Your answers to these questions provide the basis for the recommendations produced by your research.

End of a journey?

You have travelled a long way, from deciding a topic, investigating it and generating findings and recommendations. Along this road you have (I hope) taken notes and written drafts for your written project. Now you must turn all this into a polished product, ready to be shared with your tutor, marked by your marker, and – perhaps – read and discussed by professional colleagues eager to learn from what you have discovered. 'Writing up' is your final, very important task – we deal with it now.

Further reading 📖

Adelman, C. (ed.) (1981) *Uttering, Muttering: Collecting, Using and Reporting Talk for Social and Educational Research*. London: Grant McIntyre.
A classic text on listening to and using people's talk as data for your research.

Denscombe, M. (2010) *The Good Research Guide*. 4th ed. Maidenhead: Open University Press.
I recommend Chapter 13 of this book for its careful explanation of basic concepts relating to analysis of quantitative data, its guidance on how to work with descriptive statistics and its advice on presentation of findings in charts, tables and text.

Menter, I., Elliot, D., Hulme, M., Lewin, J. and Lowden, K. (2011) *A Guide to Practitioner Research in Education*. London: Sage.
Part 5 of this book provides a clear and useful examination of how quantitative and qualitative data can be analysed and presented.

Richard, L. (2009) *Handling Qualitative Data: A Practical Guide*. 2nd ed. London: Sage.
This book covers the use of qualitative data as a whole, but is especially strong on the processes of recording and analysis.

12 Writing up your project

What will you learn from this chapter?

You now need to write up your research, so you can share it with others. This chapter takes you through this whole process, with plenty of advice, big and small, along the way.

First tasks

There are several important tasks first of all:

- **Project requirements**: First check the requirements for presentation of your project as stated in your course documentation:
  - How many words should you write? Does this word count include direct quotations? Appendices? Everything?
  - How should the text be structured? What sections should it have? What appendices should it include?
  - Should the research venue and participants remain anonymous in the text? (Probably, yes.)
- **Assessment criteria**: Then examine the assessment criteria which show how your project will be marked and graded. Keep in mind the criteria for top or 'A' grades – these are what you should be aiming to achieve.
- **Reading**: Examine research written by others – dissertations held in your library, collections of papers or journal articles. Look at structure and style, especially how writers seek to achieve the elements described in this chapter.
- **Backing up**: Back up what you write: on a server, another computer, memory stick, or all of these. Losing work is soul-destroying, and it happens!

Project framework

Your course documentation may stipulate that you organize your written project in several separate sections. You must be clear about what each of these is about. We will now work through a framework which is probably similar, but not identical, to that which you may need to follow. You will find that the Project Sheets you have completed while working through this book will give you an excellent basis for writing many sections.

Title page

Your project probably needs a front page, showing the title, your name as the author, and the name of the institution where you are a student. You may also need to confirm on this page that the work is your own and has not been previously submitted for assessment.

Abstract

An abstract is a short (roughly 200 words), concise summary of the topic, methods and main findings of your investigation. Note that it is a summary of your research, not an introduction to it (researchers often read abstracts and nothing more – some readers of your project may do the same). Check the accuracy of your abstract last, when everything else is finished – make sure that what is written matches your project as a whole. You can write it in either the past or present tense, but do not change tenses half-way through. Technical terms or jargon may need a very concise explanation. Examine the abstracts of articles in research journals to see how they are done. You may also need to provide 'keywords' reflecting your project's main themes.

Acknowledgements

This section allows you to thank those who have helped with your project, for instance: staff, children and students at your research venue; other participants; your project tutor; family and friends. Keep acknowledgements brief and remember not to identify individuals or your research venue by name.

Contents

You may need to include a contents page, giving section titles and the first page number of each. Look at the contents page of this book to see how this is done. You may also require separate lists of figures and tables, giving the title and page number of each.

Research issue

You may now be asked to describe concisely what your research is about. If you did Activity 9.2 in Chapter 9, you may already have a useful statement which you can use. Here again, you may wish to include a short explanation of key terminology, so that your reader understands your project properly from the very start.

Justification

Here you explain why the issue you investigated was considered worthy of research. You could provide several reasons (as suggested in Chapter 4 and Project Sheet 2):

1 **International, national or local significance:** Explain why your topic was considered important for education in a general sense, or specifically in relation to your research venue. Support your explanation by referring to key documents, such as a government report, or to wider literature.
2 **Professional relevance:** Explain also how your investigation informs your professional understanding and practice. If relevant, say too how your project helps you towards competency standards associated with your course.
3 **Personal interest:** Explain why the topic interested you personally.

Research questions

It is now time to present your research questions. You should have a draft of these from Project Sheet 4, refined at intervals on Project Sheet 5. You could also explain how they reflect features of effective research questions recommended in the research literature. You must be very sure that your questions match what you have investigated in your research. Number them so that you can easily refer to them in later parts of your project.

Literature review

This will normally take up about a quarter of the word count for the project as a whole. It should provide a clear analytical picture of what is (or is not) known already about your topic and about wider issues of which your topic is a part. Here is some guidance, some of it a reminder of advice from Chapter 6:

• Think carefully about structure, reflecting perhaps that which you set out in Project Sheet 7. If this is the case, start with broader themes, including further discussion of key concepts if necessary. Move in stages towards examination of literature closely related to the specific topic of your investigation.

- Use sub-headings to identify the different issues you discuss; make sure that ideas flow logically from one to the next.

- Use continuous prose, not bullet points or numbered lists, to present a well-ordered, interesting discussion.

- Vary the verbs you use when presenting what authors have written. For example, Smith (2012) 'argues', 'claims', 'maintains', supports', 'disputes' or 'explores'. More options are provided by Ballenger (2004: 238), or use your thesaurus (see Activity 1.1. in Chapter 1).

- Point out areas of agreement and difference, or how what one commentator says expands on or diverges from what is said by another. Find contradictions or tensions in the arguments you examine.

- Use connecting words and phrases to explain these relationships, for example: 'furthermore', 'in particular', 'nevertheless', 'similarly', 'consequently', 'in contrast', 'on the one hand', 'on the other hand' or 'to summarize' (also those already noted in Chapter 6).

- Evaluate the literature, for instance: 'Jones (2010) has argued convincingly that ...'; 'Smith's (2012) examination of this issue was limited in scope' (this rather detached style is usually better than writing 'I think that ...' or 'My view is that ...').

- Use the present or past tense, e.g. 'Smith (2012) states ...', or 'Smith (2012) stated ...', but be consistent in your choice.

- Reference all literature accurately using your required style of referencing.

- At the end of the review, summarize the main ideas which have emerged and consider their relevance for your investigation. You may be able to identify a gap in current knowledge which your research set out to fill.

Methodology

This section again requires about a quarter of your total word count. Describe the methods you used to investigate your topic and give reasons for your choice, making reference to advice in literature on doing research. You should provide exact details of what you did, who you involved (your sample) and why you chose these participants (see Project Sheet 8). A table, such as Megan's below, can be useful as part of this. You should also describe the research instruments you used (questionnaire, interview questions, observation framework) and you may need to include them in appendices. You should also make clear how you analysed your data – it is important for readers to understand this too. Re-read Chapters 7, 8 and 11 to make sure you approach this task well and also look at methodology sections in published research articles.

Megan presents details of her research

Megan has carried out a questionnaire and interviews for her investigation into the teaching of three-dimensional shapes. She presents her data-collection events in this chart:

Date	Nature of data collection	Sample	Duration (mins)	Notes
17 March	Observation of mathematics lesson	Class C, 25 children. Observation focused on group of 4 children (2 female + 2 male)	45	Written notes taken
17 March	Group interview	Group of 4 children observed earlier	15	Children completed task as part of interview
19 March	Individual interview	Teacher from observed mathematics lesson	30	Interview voice-recorded

Figure 12.1 Megan's data-collection events

Validity and reliability

You may need to consider validity and reliability within your methodology section, or separately. Define the terms, drawing from literature on doing research, and identify particular threats relating to your investigation. Say what steps you took to lessen these threats and to strengthen the validity and reliability of your research (see Chapter 9 and Project Sheet 12).

Ethics

You may need to consider ethics in all sections, or in a section of its own. Either way, you should examine the particular ethical issues relating to your investigation and the steps you took to deal with these, again using research literature to inform your discussion. Several Project Sheets are relevant here, especially Project Sheet 13.

Presentation and analysis of data

Here you present and analyse the data you collected. Again, up to a quarter of your word count will be needed, perhaps including the discussion which follows. Here are some suggestions for this vital part of your project:

- Use your research questions as sub-headings, then clearly present and analyse data against each of these questions in turn (this reflects the way you organized your data in Chapter 11).

- Explain your data in your text, and be exact when you do so. Avoid relying on approximations such as 'most', 'few', 'often' – give exact numbers or percentages as well or instead. For example: 'A large majority of respondents (89%) indicated that …'.

- If necessary (they may not be), incorporate tables or charts. Refer your reader to these, for instance: 'Full data are presented in Table 7.2'. Hannah, in Chapter 11, used a simple table, but bar or pie charts, histograms, scatter plots and graphs are also possible, depending on the kind of data you are presenting (Denscombe, 2010: 261–267, provides useful examples). However, your first concern should be clarity, not 'looking good', so whatever you decide to use, keep it simple and effective.

- Integrate your data when answering each research question. For instance, you might present numerical data from questionnaires in a simple chart; follow this with sample quotes taken from interviews to illustrate the main emerging ideas; and finally provide document-analysis data which give alternative perspectives.

- Do not incorporate your own views or experiences – let your data do the talking.

Discussion of findings

Your analysis of data will produce findings – what exactly you have discovered, in answer to your research questions. Now you need to discuss these findings critically. What are their overall value, their strengths and weaknesses? How do they inform practice? What issues remain unclear or unresearched? Integrate your discussion – how do findings from one question link to findings from another? Remember also to relate your findings back to what you discovered in your literature review – in what ways do they match, contradict or add to what the literature told you about this issue? (See Chapter 11.) Refer also to your research questions, tracking how you have addressed them and identifying elements where findings are incomplete.

Conclusions and recommendations

Finally, you sum up the main outcomes of your research and provide recommendations emerging from these. Recommendations may relate to institutions or services, to teachers or other professionals, to researchers and to yourself (see Chapter 11 for different kinds you can provide). They must reflect the findings of your research – do not introduce new ideas or new material at this stage. Bullet-pointed or numbered lists may be acceptable, but also include a commentary to set them in context.

References

At the end of your main text, you must present a clear, complete and accurate list of references you have cited in your text. We consider this process in a separate section below.

Appendices

These may be required in your project. They provide extra information – too substantial for the main text – about your research, how you carried it out and the data you collected. They could include:

- your research brief (see Chapter 9 and Project Sheet 14)
- your signed ethical approval form (Chapter 9)
- letters (anonymized) you wrote to your research venue or to participants, asking for their consent (Chapter 10)
- your data-collection instruments, for example questionnaire, interview framework, observation framework (Chapter 8 and Project Sheets 9, 10 and 11)
- any detailed or complex quantitative data, too extensive to include within your main text
- examples of analysed qualitative data to show how you did your analysis.

Do not include large documents or examples of literature. Do not include all your raw data (unless required to do so) – these should have been summarized and analysed carefully and comprehensively in your main text. However, you should keep your raw data for a reasonable period, in case your marker or assessment board asks to see them. Each appendix should be numbered and given a title, for example: 'Appendix 1: Questionnaire for Parents'. Each should also be referred to in the body of the project, for example: 'Parents were asked about the value of homework in a questionnaire (see Appendix 1)'. Note that although appendices are important, your reader must be able to understand and appreciate your investigation and its findings without looking at them. All vital information therefore needs to be in your main text.

Academic writing

Your whole project will be composed in an 'academic writing style'. This notion can be rather intimidating, but it need not be. You will have become familiar with academic writing styles in your reading, especially if you have looked at journal articles. You will have also (I hope) practised your writing while drafting sections of your text, and by doing so improved along the way.

Academic writing is formal (but not pompously so), and should also (surprisingly) be 'reader-friendly'. This 'reader-friendliness' comes not from fancy styles and impenetrable vocabulary, but from a coherent and logical structure and precise, analytical writing. Here are three elements which are very important for this:

* **Understandability**: Think: who are your readers? You can presume that they have reasonable general knowledge about the world, education and research, and that they understand long words and critical argument. However, presume too that they are not experts in the educational issue you have chosen to investigate, or indeed in the minutiae of research itself. You therefore need to explain concepts and terminology, so they can properly comprehend and appreciate your work. Whether or not the marker of your project is an expert in one or both of these respects, your explanations will be evidence of your own understanding, and this is likely to be an important element in assessment of what you have achieved.

* **Consistency**: The last thing your readers want is for you to keep changing your mind. You must therefore make sure that every time you describe your research, you do so in the same way – not necessarily with identical words, but expressing a consistent idea of what your project is about.

* **Precision**: Vagueness is another enemy of good academic writing. Your explanations must be concise and clear; discussion must be balanced and objective; arguments must arise from an evaluation of literature and analysis of data, not from your own personal opinions, emotions or experiences; and conclusions and recommendations must be logically reached.

Plagiarism

We should add another quality of academic writing to these: **responsibility**. The written project, and the investigation itself, must be your own. It must not be 'plagiarized', that is, presented as your own work when in fact it is someone else's. Plagiarism is a serious wrongdoing in research and academic writing and, if discovered, consequences are severe.

So, read the work of others and take on ideas about how to improve, but remember throughout that composition of your project is ultimately your own responsibility. It is your investigation, your writing, and when you draw ideas or quotations from elsewhere, you must reference these to show where they have come from (see below). Beware also of sharing your own writing too freely with others – you will not be pleased if someone else plagiarizes your hard work. To learn more about this important issue, search for films about plagiarism at Vimeo: http://vimeo/heacademy, or on YouTube.

Referencing

A vital part of avoiding plagiarism is to reference fully and accurately. It means acknowledging clearly where the ideas which you describe, use and discuss have originated. Referencing also shows that you have read widely and based your research on the wealth of understanding built up by other writers and researchers. Good referencing is an essential part of your written project.

Remember to check which referencing system is used by your place of study. Whichever system it is, it is likely that online or printed guidance on its use will be available to you. Alternatively, you could consult Neville (2010) which covers a range of referencing styles. The advice which I give here reflects the Harvard system, in which there are two elements to consider: referencing (or 'citing') within the text, and producing a list of references at the end. We now deal with each in turn.

Referencing within the text

When citing a piece of literature within your text, the normal method is to give the author's family name, followed by the year of publication. If the reference is used as part of a sentence, then the date goes in brackets, for example: 'Smith (2012) claimed that good educators are made, not born'. If it is not part of the sentence, but added to it after the idea it relates to, then the whole reference goes in brackets: 'It has been claimed that good educators are made, not born (Smith, 2012).' Note that here the full stop goes right at the end, after the closing bracket. If two pieces of literature by different authors share the same name and date, then add the authors' initials in the text as well, to distinguish between the two (you may have noticed 'C. Robson (2011)' and 'S. Robson (2011)' in Chapters 7 and 8 where I did this).

Online material may have no date. There are two ways you can handle this:

- Use 'n.d.' to denote 'no date'. For instance: 'Smith (n.d.) stated …'.
- Estimate the date and follow it with a question mark, for example: 'Smith (2012?) stated that …'.

Providing a reference list

You will provide a list of all the material cited in your text at the end of your project. There are important rules to follow for this:

- Present all references in *one* alphabetical list, as in the reference list at the end of this book. Do not list online material separately, for example.

- Your list must include *all* material you cited in the text. Do not miss anything out.

- It should *only* include material cited in your text. Do not include material you have read, but not cited in your text.

- The author and date provided in your text must match the author and date you provide in your list. For example, if in your text you cite 'British Broadcasting Corporation (2010)', the reference in your list must start in the same way, not 'BBC (2010)'.

- If two references have the same author and date, add 'a' and 'b' to the date, for instance, Smith (2012a) and Smith (2012b) to tell them apart. Do this in the text and the reference list.

The following are examples of references for such a list. Look carefully at how they are set out (author's family name, initials, date in brackets, etc.) and use them (as well as the reference list at the end of this book) as a guide. Note that online references should also include the date you 'accessed' or looked at them – this is because online material can change over time.

Book: Lambert, M. (2012) *A Beginner's Guide to Doing Your Education Research Project.* London: Sage.

Chapter in book: Torrance, H. (2004) 'Using action research to generate knowledge about educational practice', in G. Thomas, and R. Pring (eds) *Evidence-Based Practice in Education.* Maidenhead: Open University Press.

Journal article: Bartram, B. and Bailey, C. (2009) 'Different students, same difference?: A comparison of UK and international students' understandings of "effective teaching"', *Active Learning in Higher Education*, 10(2): 172–184.

Online source: Kennedy, J.F. (1961) Inaugural address. [Online] www. bartleby.com/124/pres56.html (accessed 13 July 2012).

 Activity 12.1   Find the referencing mistakes

Here is a short piece of text and its reference list. Find the referencing mistakes (there are at least 12). The answers are in Appendix II.

(Continued)

(Continued)

Swan (2009) wrote that observations are a useful way of getting information about classroom practice. However, Finch warned that it is difficult to decide what to watch. Researchers need to plan in advance (Crow, 2010). Chickadee (2011) suggested drawing up a chart which could be filled in during the observation. As Wren C. (2009) advised: 'When you observe, you need to work out exactly what it is you want to find out.'

Crow, A. (2010) *Research in the Classroom.*

Finch, P. (2008) *Investigating for You.* Boston: Fledgling Books.

Swan, W. (2008) *An Introduction to Research.* Nonsuch Publications: Sydney.

Swift, S. and Jay H. (2006) *Planning your Research.* [Online] www.research&resources.com (accessed 13 February).

Chickadee (2011) *Carrying out Effective Observations.* London: Binocular Press.

Wren, C. 'Researching my way', in A. Bush (ed.) *How to Succeed in Teacher Research.* New York: Twitcher Books.

Extra guidance

The more you reference, the more there is to learn about it. Here is some extra guidance:

Secondary referencing: Sometimes you wish to cite in your text a piece of literature which you find described elsewhere. For instance, Smith (2012) describes the work of Jones (2010), and you want to draw on what Jones said in your project. This is called 'secondary referencing'. In this case, in your text you can write: 'Jones (2010, in Smith, 2012) suggested that ...'. In your reference list, give the reference for Smith (2012), not the reference for Jones (2010) – your readers can go to Smith's book if they wish to see that.

Multiple authors: When a publication has two authors, give both their names when citing their literature in your text, for instance: Smith and Brown (2011). If there are more than two, you can write the first name, then: '*et al.*', which means 'and others', for example: Green *et al.* (2011). In research papers this is usually written in italics: *et al.* . List the names of all the authors in your reference list.

Page numbers: Provide page numbers for direct quotations used in your text, or if you wish to pinpoint exactly where a particular idea is described. There are various ways of doing this; for example:

- Smith (2012: 31) stated: 'Educators are made, not born'.
- Smith stated: 'Educators are made, not born' (2012: 31).
- Smith (2012) stated: 'Educators are born, not made' (p. 31).
- Smith (2012, p. 31) stated: 'Educators are born, not made'.

Whichever system you choose, use it consistently throughout your text. If a quotation stretches over two pages, give both, for example: Smith (2012: 35–36). If you are quoting from a publication with no page number (for example, Internet material), give the section number (if there is one) or the section title to show where the quotation comes from, for example: 'Educators are made, not born' (Smith, 2012: Section 3.1).

Bibliography: A bibliography is a list of all the material you have looked at while working on your project, or which you recommend for further reading. It is not the same as a reference list. Most projects do not require a bibliography. To be sure, check your course requirements.

Writing well

According to Hart (1998: 11), 'it takes considerable effort and time to express ideas in writing'. Patience, commitment and a strong desire for clarity could be added to this list. Below is further guidance to help you through this task. There may be online or face-to-face study skills support available at your place of study to assist you further.

Structure

- **Headings and sub-headings**: Use headings and sub-headings to organize your text systematically and clearly. Decide on a logical system: for instance, main headings in bold upper case; sub-headings in bold lower case. You could also use numbers, for example: 1, then 1.1 (the activities in this book are numbered in this way).
- **Forewarnings and summaries**: Include in each section an introductory paragraph (forewarning what is to come) and a concluding paragraph (summarizing the main outcomes of the section). This helps your reader to 'stay with you' as you progress through your project.
- **Quotations**: Use direct quotations (from the literature or from your data) to illustrate ideas and arguments discussed in your text. In general, keep them short and integrate them into your text, as I did when quoting Hart (1998) above.
- **Word count**: Keep to your required word count, and make sure the length of sections reflects their relative importance.

Style

- **Past tense**: You have now carried out your research, so write in the past tense.

- **Restraint**: Remain reserved and circumspect in your judgements. Avoid, for example: 'It is obvious that ...' and 'Everyone can see that ...'. Instead, write: 'It seems clear that ...' or 'It can be concluded that ...'.

- **Confidence**: You should, however, be assertive about the aims and general outcomes of your project. Do not write: 'This project aimed to examine ...' or 'Outcomes of this research will hopefully inform ...'. Write instead: 'This project examined ...' and 'Outcomes inform ...'.

- **Personalization**: Some writers (and tutors) dislike this kind of sentence: 'This project investigates the teaching of reading'. They argue that it is not the project which 'investigates', rather it is you, the researcher. However, others do not find it a problem, and I have often used this kind of phrase in this book.

- **'I' and 'my'**: Opinions also vary on the use of 'I' and 'my' in research texts. My view is that it is sometimes reasonable to write in this way, for instance when justifying your topic or evaluating your research (the project is yours, after all). In the middle sections, however, when writing about the literature, the investigation and the data produced, a less personalized style is usually preferable. In general, do not overuse 'I' and 'my' – find other ways of writing too.

Vocabulary

Anonymity: Remember this promise to your participants. Change or disguise names, and do your best not to give information which means they could be identified by other means.

Restraint (again): Avoid words like 'fantastic', 'terrible' – use more detached vocabulary. Be cautious, in particular, with your choice of verbs. Avoid these: 'show'; 'demonstrate'; and, especially, 'prove'. 'Suggest' or 'indicate' are better options.

Gender: Avoid stereotyping. For example, do not refer to all teachers as 'he', or all children as 'she'. Instead, use 'he or she', 's/he', or 'they' to denote both genders.

'Significant': This word has a technical meaning associated with the analysis of quantitative data. Use 'considerable', 'meaningful' or 'important' instead.

'Includes': Sometimes you wish to make use of a long list of elements from the literature, for instance a list of recommended teaching resources. Repeating everything would take too many words and would frankly be rather boring. The word 'includes' can help you here, for instance: 'Smith's (2012) list of recommended teaching resources includes maps, satellite images and a range of Internet materials'. Or: 'Among the resources recommended by Smith (2012) are ...' This shows that you are aware of the resources you have not listed and indicates a degree of criticality because you have had to choose which to mention.

Abbreviations: In the text, provide the full term followed by the abbreviation in brackets the first time you use it, for example: 'Department for Education (DfE)'. After that, the abbreviation will usually suffice. You may be asked to provide a list of abbreviations and their meanings at the start of your project.

Grammar and punctuation

Full sentences: Write in full sentences. What constitutes a 'full sentence' is not always easy to define (see Chapter 4 of Cameron, 2007, for an interesting discussion), but for the writing of your project it means a set of words starting with a capital letter, ending in a full stop, and including at least a subject and verb (in most cases an object too). Avoid beginning sentences with 'And' or 'But'.

Although/however: Avoid 'although' at the start of a short sentence too, for example: 'Although this is not supported by other evidence.'. This is a phrase, rather than a complete sentence. Instead, join the phrase to the previous sentence using a comma: 'Jones (2010) offers a strong opinion, although this is not supported by other evidence.'. Or start the sentence with 'However' instead: 'However, this is not supported by other evidence.'.

Contractions: Avoid 'don't', 'isn't', 'can't', etc. Write 'do not', 'is not', 'cannot' instead.

Quotations: Direct quotations from the literature do not need to be in italics or bold. Enclose them within single (') or double (") inverted commas – be consistent in which you use. If you need to use inverted commas within a quotation, use the kind you have not used for the quotation as a whole, for instance: Smith (2012: 13) suggested that 'a key factor is development of what are known as "community" or "local" values'. Quotations longer than three or four lines (or 40 words) are normally indented (set in from the edges of your text) without inverted commas.

Spelling

Correct spelling is 'a must'. Different usage in the UK and the USA complicates the process: check your computer spell-check is properly set, but note that, even so, mistakes can go unnoticed. The most common are associated with confusion of related or similar terms, for example:

Practice/practise: In UK English, 'practice' is the noun, 'practise' the verb. So: 'Children practise spelling every day' and 'Spelling practice takes place every day'. In American English, 'practice' is used for both.

Effect/affect: In nearly all cases, 'effect' is the noun, 'affect' is the verb. So: 'The effect is unclear' and 'This affects what is done'.

Principal/principle: 'Principal' is usually an adjective, meaning main or most important (although the head of a college may be 'the Principal'). 'Principle' is a noun, meaning a rule or theory.

Its/it's: 'Its' is a possessive, like his or her. 'It's' (with an apostrophe) is short for 'it is', so if you avoid contractions (see above), it will never be used in your project, unless quoted from interview or other data.

Apostrophes

Misuse of apostrophes is the most common mistake of all. This may not matter in some contexts, but in your project it does. Here are some basic rules:

- When there is one owner, the apostrophe goes before the 's': 'The teacher's book' (the book belongs to one teacher).
- When there is more than one owner, the apostrophe goes after the 's': 'The teachers' book' (it belongs to more than one teacher).
- When the singular word ends in 's', the apostrophe goes after the 's': 'James' book'.
- When the plural word does not end in 's', the apostrophe goes after the word followed by 's': 'The children's book'.

If you are still unclear, read (and be entertained by) *Eats, Shoots and Leaves*, by Lynne Truss – see further reading below.

 Activity 12.2   Find the mistakes

There are 12 mistakes in this passage. Can you find them all? The correct text is in Appendix II.

How does teaching effect student's learning? Is practise the most affective method? Students are different – one students way of learning is not the way of other students. It depends who's opinion you listen too. Childrens' learning is very complicated, so the principle concern for a school is to pay attention to it's work so that its student's can learn succesfully.

Proofreading

Your aim should be to produce a fully accurate text, nothing less. Proofreading – careful checking of grammar, spelling, referencing and overall clarity – can help you reach this aim. Do it yourself, but ask someone else to do it too, preferably someone who writes accurately themselves. They will find mistakes which you have missed. If you can afford it, you could pay a professional proofreader to do the job – search on the Internet for these services, or ask at your place of study.

 Activity 12.3   Self-evaluate your project

If I was marking your project, I would be looking for these main elements:

- an interesting and valuable topic
- well-phrased research questions, consistently addressed throughout the project
- an interesting, analytical review of the relevant literature
- carefully designed and piloted methodology and research instruments
- close consideration of validity, reliability (possibly), and ethics
- detailed data and persuasive analysis, as a result of 'digging deep'
- findings and conclusions logically drawn from this analysis
- relevant recommendations of value to education and to continuing research
- clear, concise and accurate writing throughout.

How does your project fare against these criteria? What are its strengths? What are its weaknesses? Can you, before you hand it in, address any of those weaknesses? If not, can you acknowledge and discuss them in your project? No investigation is perfect, but weaknesses are lessened if the researcher recognizes them and shares them with their reader.

Presentation

Your place of study should give you guidance on how to present your project and submit it for assessment. Here are some elements which are often required:

- Word-process your text, printing on one side of the paper only.
- Start a new page for each main section.
- Double-space or 1.5-space the text (leave an extra line space between paragraphs).
- Leave margins on the left and right of your text for your marker's comments.
- Insert page numbers and your name and student number as a footer to each page.
- Bind your project (comb-binding is usually appropriate).
- Submit your project by the required hand-in date (you may need to submit two copies).
- Keep a separate copy for yourself.
- Note that you may be required to submit your project electronically as well as or instead of submitting it in print.

Further reading

American Psychological Association (2010) *Publication Manual of the American Psychological Association*. 6th ed. Washington, DC: American Psychological Association.

When you come up against particularly thorny problems of presentation, style or referencing, this is the manual to consult. It is the ultimate communication guide for writers on both sides of the Atlantic, and a good book for settling arguments.

Fielding, N. and Allen, J. (2006) 'Writing dissertations, theses and reports', in N. Gilbert (ed.) *From Postgraduate to Social Scientists: A Guide to Key Skills*. London: Sage.

Directed at postgraduate students, this guide offers very useful advice for undergraduates too. It includes help on each section of a written project, similar to (but not the same as) my suggestions here. The subsequent chapter, 'Writing articles, books and presentations', by Rowena Murray, will also help you, especially if you wish to publish your research more widely, as I discuss in the conclusion to this book.

Hyatt, D. (2004) 'Writing research?', in C. Opie (ed.) *Doing Educational Research: A Guide for First Time Researchers*. London: Sage.

This chapter too is aimed at Masters-level researchers, but undergraduates doing research will also learn from Hyatt's clear advice.

Seely, J. (2005) *Oxford Guide to Effective Writing and Speaking*. 2nd ed. Oxford: Oxford University Press.

This book provides guidance on many types of communication in English, including presentations, essays, projects and dissertations. Topics include grammar, spelling and the writing process, with examples and exercises to improve your accuracy and skills.

Truss, L. (2003) *Eats, Shoots and Leaves: The Zero Tolerance Approach to Punctuation.* London: Profile Books.
I recommended this in the text, and I list it here too. It is a best-selling treatise and guide on the use of punctuation – and enjoyable enough (like the Phinn books I recommended in Chapter 10) to read on the beach.

 BBC: www.bbc.co.uk/skillswise/words/grammar

This and other BBC web pages offer a range of resources for improving writing skills.

Conclusion

You hand in your project – and understandably breathe a sigh of relief. You wait, perhaps nervously, for feedback and, if relevant, your grade. Take a break by all means (you deserve it), but there are some further important issues to consider in relation to your project.

Viva?

A 'viva' (an abbreviation of 'viva voce', meaning 'by living voice') is an oral examination where you present your project to examiners and explain, debate and 'defend' what you have done and written. If and when you write a doctoral thesis, you will attend a viva, and it is sometimes required for other kinds of research too. If this applies to you, your sigh of relief is short-lived. The good news is, however, that your viva is likely to be a rewarding, even exhilarating, extra challenge.

The big positive is that you know your project better than your examiners and can therefore talk much better about it than they can. Nevertheless, ring-fence quality time beforehand so you can prepare for your viva well:

- Read your written project once again, so it is fresh in your mind.
- Keep an eye out for new research or news stories relating to your topic, appearing since you finished your project.
- Think about what questions you might be asked and rehearse answers to these.
- Do a 'mock' or practice viva beforehand (your project tutor may be ready to help you with this).

Here are some questions which you could be asked:

- *What have you learnt from your project? How does it contribute to wider knowledge and understanding in education?*
- *The justification for your topic is fairly brief. Can you say more about why you chose it?*
- *In your project, you mention Smith's (2012) criticism of this approach. How do you answer such criticism?*
- *If you did your project again, what would you do differently?*

Here is a strategy for answering these and other questions, informed by Murray's (2009) very helpful guide:

1 Start your answer by explaining what is in your written project, for example: 'In my project, I wrote that ...' ; 'The approach I took in my project was ...'.

2 Then move on to considering wider relevant issues, for instance:

- Discuss your actual experiences of doing research and what you learnt from these.

- Update what you wrote in your project, perhaps drawing on more recent research relating to your topic.

- Discuss arguments for and against the issue under discussion, and present your own position.

- Apply the outcomes of your research to educational developments not considered in your project. For instance, how does your research about teaching history relate to debate about what a history curriculum should include?

 Zara's viva

Examiners: *With hindsight, how do you view your choice of methods in your research?*

Zara: *In my project I explain that I used questionnaires to give a wide spectrum of opinion on my topic, and interviews to add depth to what I found out. In general terms this was true, but looking back, I realize that the questionnaire was not as successful as it could have been. When analysing responses I found that one or two questions had been understood by respondents in different ways, and the data were therefore difficult to deal with. If I did my research again, I would focus even more closely on piloting the questionnaire, perhaps more than once, to refine its design.*

Saying thank you

Many people have supported you while doing your project: your tutor, family, friends. You will find a simple way of thanking them, I am sure. You may also wish to thank those who have contributed to your data collection in various ways – children, students, staff and others. The straightforward approach is to say it, but you could consider doing other things as well:

- **Presenting gifts:** Pens or crayons for a class of children or chocolates for helpful parents or staff might be appropriate. This is the right time to do this, when all your data collection is complete – giving a gift during your investigation can disturb your relationship with participants, who may then feel a sense of obligation towards you.

- **Providing input:** Sharing the outcomes of your research can be a valuable way of giving something back in return for help. You could, for instance, send participants a written summary of your research outcomes, or offer to discuss your research findings at a staff meeting.

- **Writing a letter:** A good way to say thank you is to write a letter to the head or manager of your research venue. They can then share it with governors, inspectors or others, as positive evidence of the venue's interest in research and improvement. In the letter, thank in general terms everyone who has helped, and mention individuals by name only if this does not breach promises of anonymity which you made. Keep everything brief and concise – and accurately written, of course.

- **Keeping in touch:** Your venue may also like to know the grade you receive (especially if it is a high one) and how it contributed to your course outcomes as a whole. Beyond that, remember that their work moves on (as does yours) and your relationship with your research venue may fade over time. If you have made a good impression, however, there will always be staff who remember you with respect, and this may benefit you as your career in education continues to develop.

Dissemination

There is one other question to consider at this stage, especially if your project has received positive feedback. How could the outcomes of your project be disseminated further? Doing this gives others the opportunity to learn from your investigation and to use your findings to inform their professional practice. On a personal level, it is also hugely rewarding and can be a positive career move. Here are some options:

Poster: If you have discussed your research at a staff meeting, as suggested above, a 'poster presentation' at a conference or other event is a useful next step. You need to prepare a clear and concise display about your project and be prepared to discuss your research with conference delegates who visit your 'stand'.

Conference paper: Giving a formal conference paper is a further step. You will need to adapt your text, shorten and possibly re-structure it to bring out the main points and raise issues for further debate. Most conferences invite abstracts and use them to choose which papers to include in the programme. Your project tutor may be willing to help you find a suitable event.

In print: Imagine seeing your project in print. Again, further work will be needed – for instance, you will need to reduce the length of your text and strengthen weaker aspects where possible. If you are prepared to tackle this, your project could end up as:

- an item in a professional newsletter, published by a subject association or voluntary organization
- an item on an education or research website
- an article in a professional or academic journal
- a chapter in a book on the general topic of your research
- part of a collection of research projects, perhaps similar to those published at my own place of work (Lambert and Hollinshead, 2004; Mycroft, 2011; Mycroft et al., 2010).

Learning from your research

Readers of your work should not be the only ones to learn from your research. Most of all, you should (and will) do so yourself. Here are three benefits you will have gained, which will stand you in good stead as your work and career in education continue to progress:

- You have learnt more about your chosen topic. You now understand your practice better and have the chance to improve it.
- You have learnt how to investigate any topic in depth, a vital skill to have in education.
- Along the way, you have made many decisions, solved many problems, and perhaps had to live with a few mistakes as well. You have become more independent, resourceful and assured as a result.

Doing research is a journey travelled – I hope that yours was both successful and rewarding. If you decide to undertake further investigation, for instance for a higher degree, you will gain even more. If you have worked through this book to its end, and completed your project well, you can now do so not as a beginner, but as a practised and capable researcher.

References

Alderson, P. (2004) 'Ethics', in S. Fraser, V. Lewis, S. Ding, M. Kellett and C. Robinson (eds) *Doing Research with Children and Young People*. London: Sage.

Alderson, P. and Morrow, V. (2011) *The Ethics of Research with Children and Young People: A Practical Handbook*. London: Sage.

Anderson, G. and Arsenault, N. (1998) *Fundamentals of Educational Research*. 2nd ed. London: Falmer Press.

Ballenger, B. (2004) *The Curious Researcher: A Guide to Writing Research Papers*. 4th ed. New York: Pearson Education.

Barbour, R. and Schostak, J. (2005) 'Interviewing and focus groups', in B. Somekh, and C. Lewin (eds) *Research Methods in the Social Sciences*. London: Sage.

Basit, T.N. (2010) *Conducting Research in Educational Contexts*. London: Continuum.

Bazeley, P. (2007) *Qualitative Data Analysis with NVivo*. London: Sage.

Birley, G. and Moreland, N. (1998) *A Practical Guide to Academic Research*. London: Kogan.

Blatchford, P., Bassett, P., Brown, P., Martin, C., Russell, A. and Webster, R. (2011) 'The impact of support staff on pupils' "positive approaches to learning" and their academic progress', *British Educational Research Journal*, 37(3): 443–464.

Blaxter, L., Hughes, C. and Tight, M. (2001) *How to Research*. 2nd ed. Buckingham: Open University Press.

Blaxter, L., Hughes, C. and Tight, M. (2010) *How to Research*. 4th ed. Maidenhead: Open University Press.

Blenkinsop, S., Bradshaw, S., Cade, J., Chan, D., Greenwood, D., Ransley, J., Schagen, S., Scott, E., Teeman, D. and Thomas, J. (2007) *Further Evaluation of the School Fruit and Vegetable Scheme*. London: Department of Health.

Callan, E. (2011) 'When to shut students up: civility, silencing, and free speech', *Theory and Research in Education*, 9(1): 3–22.

Cameron, D. (2007) *The Teacher's Guide to Grammar*. Oxford: Oxford University Press.

Clark, A. and Moss, P. (2005) *Spaces to Play: More Listening to Young Children Using the Mosaic Approach*. London: National Children's Bureau.

Denscombe, M. (2010) *The Good Research Guide*. 4th ed. Maidenhead: Open University Press.

Department for Education and Skills (2001) *Special Educational Needs: Code of Practice*. London: Department for Education and Skills.

Dunne, M., Pryor, J. and Yates, P. (2005) *Becoming a Researcher: A Research Companion for the Social Sciences*. Maidenhead: Open University Press.

Feiler, A. and Watson, D. (2010) 'Involving children with learning and communication difficulties: the perspectives of teachers, speech and language therapists and teaching assistants', *British Journal of Learning Disabilities*, 39: 113–120.

Forrester, M.A. (2010) 'Emerging musicality during the pre-school years: a case study of one child', *Psychology of Music*, 38(2): 131–158.

Friese, S. (2011) *Qualitative Data Analysis with ATLAS.ti*. London: Sage.

Galton, M., Simon, B. and Croll, P. (1980) *Inside the Primary Classroom*. London: Routledge and Kegan Paul.

Geertz, C. (2000) *The Interpretation of Cultures*. 2nd ed. New York: Basic Books.

Glaser, B.G. and Strauss, A.L. (1967) *The Discovery of Grounded Theory: Strategies for Qualitative Research*. London: Weidenfeld and Nicolson.

Gray, D.E. (2009) *Doing Research in the Real World*. 2nd ed. London: Sage.

Hammersley, M. (ed.) (2007) *Educational Research and Evidence-Based Practice*. Milton Keynes: Open University Press/London: Sage.

Hargreaves, D.H. (2007) 'Teaching as a research-based profession: possibilities and prospects (The Teacher Training Agency Lecture 1996)', in M. Hammersley (ed.) *Educational Research and Evidence-Based Practice*. Milton Keynes: Open University Press/London: Sage.

Hart, C. (1998) *Doing a Literature Review: Releasing the Social Science Research Imagination*. London: Sage.

Hill, M. (2005) 'Ethical considerations in researching children's experiences', in S. Greene and D. Hogan (eds) *Researching Children's Perspectives: Approaches and Methods*. London: Sage.

Hopkins, D. (2008) *A Teacher's Guide to Classroom Research*. Maidenhead: Open University Press.

Iivonen, S., Sääkslahti, A. and Nissinen, K. (2011) 'The development of fundamental motor skills of four- to five-year-old preschool children and the effects of a preschool physical education curriculum', *Early Child Development and Care*, 181(3): 335–343.

Jerman, J. and Pretnar, T. (2006) 'Comparative analysis of musical abilities of 11-year-olds from Slovenia and the island of Martinique', *Education 3–13*, 34(3): 233–242.

Kelly, A. and Saunders, N. (2010) 'New heads on the block: three case studies of transition to primary school headship', *School Leadership and Management*, 30(2): 127–142.

Lambert, M. and Hollinshead, A. (eds) (2004) *Raising Achievement through Teacher Research: A Collection of Teachers' Research Projects from 'Best Practice Research Scholarships'*. University of Wolverhampton, UK.

Lewis, I. and Munn, P. (2004) *So You Want to Do Research! A Guide for Beginners on How to Formulate Research Questions*. Revised ed. Glasgow: The SCRE Centre.

Lofland, J., Snow, D.A., Anderson, L. and Lofland, L.H. (2006) *Analyzing Social Settings: A Guide to Qualitative Observation and Analysis*. 4th ed. Belmont, CA: Wadsworth/Thomson Learning.

McCulloch, G. (2004) *Documentary Research: In Education, History and the Social Sciences*. London: RoutledgeFalmer.

Macintyre, C. (2000) *The Art of Action Research in the Classroom*. London: David Fulton.

Masson, J. (2004) 'The legal context', in S. Fraser, V. Lewis, S. Ding, M. Kellett and C. Robinson (eds) *Doing Research with Children and Young People*. London: Sage.

Menter, I., Elliot, D., Hulme, M., Lewin, J. and Lowden, K. (2011) *A Guide to Practitioner Research in Education*. London: Sage.

Muijs, D. (2011) *Doing Qualitative Research in Education with SPSS*. 2nd ed. London: Sage.

Mukherji, P. and Albon, D. (2010) *Research Methods in Early Childhood: An Introductory Guide*. London: Sage.

Murray, R. (2009) *How to Survive Your Viva: Defending a Thesis in an Oral Examination*. 2nd ed. Maidenhead: Open University Press.

Mycroft, L. (ed.) (2011) *Reflections on Research, Volume 2*. University of Wolverhampton, UK.

Mycroft, L., Lambert, M. and Serf, J. (eds) (2010) *Reflections on Research*. University of Wolverhampton, UK.

Neville, C. (2010) *The Complete Guide to Referencing and Avoiding Plagiarism*. 2nd ed. Maidenhead: Open University Press.

Oliver, P. (2010) *The Student's Guide to Research Ethics*. 2nd ed. Maidenhead: Open University Press.

Pollard, A. (2008) *Reflective Teaching*. 3rd ed. London: Continuum.

Pring, R. (2004) *Philosophy of Educational Research*. 2nd ed. London: Continuum.

Rassool, N. (2004) 'Flexible identities: exploring race and gender issues amongst a group of immigrant pupils in an inner-city comprehensive school', in V. Lewis, M. Kellett, C. Robinson, S. Fraser and S. Ding (eds) *The Reality of Research with Children and Young People*. London: Sage.

Read, A. and Hurford, D. (2010) '"I know how to read longer novels": developing pupils' success criteria in the classroom', *Education 3–13*, 38(1): 87–100.

Roberts-Holmes, G. (2011) *Doing Your Early Years Research Project: A Step-by-Step Guide*. 2nd ed. London: Sage.

Robson, C. (2011) *Real World Research: A Resource for Users of Social Research Methods in Applied Settings*. 3rd ed. Chichester: Wiley.

Robson, S. (2011) 'Producing and using video data with young children: a case study of ethical questions and practical consequences', in D. Harcourt, B. Perry and T. Waller (eds) *Researching Young Children's Perspectives: Debating the Ethics and Dilemmas of Educational Research with Young Children*. London: Routledge.

Rule, P. and Modipa, T.R. (2011) '"We must believe in ourselves": attitudes and experiences of adult learners with disabilities in KwaZulu-Natal, South Africa', *Adult Education Quarterly*, 28 February. Available at: http://aeq.sagepub.com/content/early/recent (accessed 27 January 2012).

Schwandt, T.A. (2003) '"Back to the rough ground": beyond theory to practice in evaluation', *Evaluation*, 9(3): 353–364.

Scott, D. (2000) *Reading Educational Research and Policy*. London: RoutledgeFalmer.

Sebba J., Crick R.D., Yu, G., Lawson H., Harlen W. and Durant K. (2008) 'Systematic review of research evidence of the impact on students in secondary schools of self and peer assessment', in *Research Evidence in Education Library*. London: EPPI-Centre, Social Science Research Unit, Institute of Education, University of London.

Sharp, J. (2009) *Success with Your Education Research Project*. Exeter: Learning Matters.

Simons, H. (2009) *Case Study Research in Practice*. London: Sage.

Taber, K.S. (2007) *Classroom-Based Research and Evidence-Based Practice: A Guide for Teachers*. London: Sage.

Tang, F. and Maxwell, S. (2007) 'Being taught to learn together: an ethnographic study of the curriculum in two Chinese kindergartens', *Early Years: An International Journal of Research and Development*, 27(2): 145–157.

Thomas, G. (2009) *How to Do Your Research Project: A Guide for Students in Education and Applied Social Sciences*. London: Sage.

Thornberg, R. (2008) 'A categorisation of school rules', *Educational Studies*, 34(1): 25–33.

Walliman, N. (2011) *Your Research Project: Designing and Planning Your Work*. 3rd ed. London: Sage.

Yin, R.K. (2009) *Case Study Research: Design and Methods*. 4th ed. London: Sage.

Appendix I
Project Sheets

These sheets are also available electronically at: www.methodspace.com/group/mikelambert. Join the group 'Mike Lambert: A Beginner's Guide'.

Project Sheet 1

Learning from other research (Chapter 3)

	Details of paper: • Author or authors • Year of publication • Title of article • Name of journal • Volume and issue numbers • Page numbers • URL and date accessed (if online)	
(a)	What is the main topic of this research? Why was this topic worth investigating?	
(b)	What specific questions did the research try to answer?	
(c)	What published material ('literature') has been used to provide the background or context to the topic being researched?	
(d)	What methods were used to collect data? Who were involved as participants?	
(e)	What does this research report say about validity, reliability and ethics?	
(f)	How were data analysed? What findings were produced?	
(g)	How might these findings inform the development of educational provision, teaching and students' learning?	
(h)	What is my/our opinion of this research? What are its strengths and weaknesses? What criticisms do I/we have of the investigation? How might it have been improved?	

Project Sheet 2

Research topic (Chapter 4)

(a)	The general topic of my research project is:
(b)	**International:** Why is it a useful topic to choose from an international perspective? How do I know? Where is it discussed?
(c)	**National:** Why is it relevant from a national perspective? What evidence do I have that this is a current issue in education: newspaper or journal article, government report, TV debate?
(d)	**Local:** Why is it important locally, or in the setting where I might carry out my investigation? What evidence do I have that this is an important issue for local professionals to address?
(e)	**Professional:** Why is it a useful topic to choose from my own professional perspective? How will it help me to strengthen my understanding and work as an educational professional? If relevant, which competency standards associated with my course will this research help me to achieve?
(f)	**Personal:** Why does the topic interest me personally?
(g)	What is the exact focus of my investigation?

Project Sheet 3

Topic checklist (Chapter 4)

	Topic of my project:		
		Yes/No/ Unsure	Notes
(a)	Does my topic meet the expectations and requirements of my course?		
(b)	Is it focused enough to explore in depth? Do I know exactly what I want to find out?		
(c)	Is it clear (test with a friend)? If not, then how do I explain or define key concepts?		
(d)	Have I got methods in mind for investigating it?		
(e)	Will I be able to arrange access to an educational setting, staff, students and others to research this topic?		
(f)	Am I sure that investigating this topic will not cause harm or distress?		
(g)	Is my topic manageable within my time frame?		
(h)	Is there 'originality' in my topic? What is it?		
(i)	What is the title of my project?		

Project Sheet 4

Research questions (Chapter 5)

(a)	The title of my research project is:
(b)	My definitions of any key terms are:
(c)	My research questions (first draft) are:
	1.
	2.
	3.

Project Sheet 5

Research question checklist (Chapter 5)

		Scrutiny 1: At the planning stage	Scrutiny 2: After my literature review	Scrutiny 3: When I start collecting data	Final scrutiny: Writing up
(a)	Are my research questions clear?				
(b)	Understandable?				
(c)	Accurate?				
(d)	Open-ended?				
(e)	Balanced and objective?				
(f)	Written in correct English?				
(g)	Have I got a rough idea about how I will find out the answers to them?				
(h)	Do I have in mind a suitable place to carry out my research?				
(i)	Are my questions manageable in relation to the time available?				
(j)	Are my questions ethical?				

A Beginner's Guide to Doing Your Education Research Project
© Mike Lambert, 2012 (SAGE)

Project Sheet 6

Identify relevant literature (Chapter 6)

	Hollie's themes	Your themes
Topic of research project ⇓	Advisory work on mathematics with classroom teachers	
Focusing out ⇓	Advisory work with teachers across the curriculum	
Focusing out ⇓	Overall responsibilities of advisers	
Widest issue	Local, regional, national and international policy on the role of advisory services	

A Beginner's Guide to Doing Your Education Research Project
© Mike Lambert, 2012 (SAGE)

Project Sheet 7

A structure for your literature review (Chapter 6)

	Hollie's themes	Your themes
Widest issue ⇓	International, national, regional and local policy on the role of advisory services	
Focusing in ⇓	Overall responsibilities of advisers	
Focusing in ⇓	Advisory work with teachers across the curriculum	
Topic of research project	Advisory work on mathematics with classroom teachers	

Project Sheet 8

Choosing methods (Chapter 7)

Method chosen	
Reasons for choosing this method (relate to literature)	
Sample chosen	
Reasons for choosing this sample (relate to literature)	
Ethical considerations?	
Practical considerations?	
What kind of data will be produced?	
Which of your research questions will these data help you to answer?	

A Beginner's Guide to Doing Your Education Research Project
© Mike Lambert, 2012 (SAGE)

Project Sheet 9

Designing a questionnaire (Chapter 8)

Title	
Who is it for?	
Introduction and instructions	
Closed questions to get factual data	
Closed question	
Open question	
Closed question	
Open question	
Closed question	
Open question	
Conclusion	

Project Sheet 10

Interview framework (Chapter 8)

Interviewee(s)	
Introduction	
Simple start (icebreakers, factual information)	
Question 1	
Question 2	
Question 3	
Question 4	
Question 5	
Question 6	
Rounding off	
Notes on how you will carry out the interview	

Project Sheet 11

Observation framework (Chapter 8)

Focus of observation				
Type of observation	Continuous	Periodic/Interval	Event-focused	Other
Notes on how the observation will be conducted				
Notes on the context of the observation				

Now enter headings, appropriate for the kind of observation you intend to carry out, in the first row of the chart below. Use the guidance in Chapter 8 for this. You can use the boxes underneath your headings for your notes when your observation is under way.

A Beginner's Guide to Doing Your Education Research Project
© Mike Lambert, 2012 (SAGE)

Project Sheet 12

Validity and reliability (Chapter 9)

Threats to objectivity	1.
	2.
	3.
Steps to strengthen validity and reliability	1.
	2.
	3.

A Beginner's Guide to Doing Your Education Research Project
© Mike Lambert, 2012 (SAGE)

Project Sheet 13

Ethics checklist (Chapter 9)

Ethical issue	Steps taken
Preserve anonymity	
Protect confidentiality	
Inform participants and others about the research	
Obtain consent	
Deal with sensitive or difficult data	
Deal with issues relating to children or other vulnerable groups	
Deal with issues relating to your own safety and welfare	
Obtain ethical approval	

Project Sheet 14

Research brief (Chapter 9)

The use of classroom routines in a primary school
Research study
Monica Jones, University of Somewhere

I am Monica Jones, a final-year student on a BA in Education course at the University of Somewhere. As part of my course, I am required to do a research project and submit a written research report.

For this project I have chosen to explore the use of routines in classrooms of children aged 5–7. My investigation involves observation of the school day, group interviews with children and individual interviews with staff. Interviews are voice-recorded (if interviewees give permission) or are summarized in written notes. My research will lead to recommendations about strengthening the use of routines as an aid to classroom management and children's learning.

All aspects of this research are carried out with the informed consent of those taking part, including children and their parents. All data are kept securely and the names of the school, staff and children will be anonymized in my research report. I will use the data collected only for purposes related to my project and university course. When I am satisfied that no further use can be made of recordings and transcripts, I will delete them.

I have approval from the Research Ethics Committee of my university to carry out this investigation. I have enhanced disclosure from the Criminal Records Bureau, indicating no convictions, cautions, reprimands and warnings. I will share relevant documentation if requested.

I will be pleased to share the results of my research with those who have kindly taken part. If you would like further information, or would like to discuss participation, please contact me (by email is best).

Monica Jones
[Contact details]

Appendix II
Activity answers

Activity 5.1: Making research questions open-ended

1 To what extent are children taught to play a musical instrument at this school?
2 What kind of training is provided for teaching assistants in this nursery?
3 In what ways do students use digital photography in geography lessons?

Activity 5.2: Making questions balanced and objective

1 What are the implications of formal tests for the education of young children?
2 What are the benefits and disadvantages for students' learning of using the college intranet?
3 In the views of staff, in what ways can the use of praise influence children's behaviour?

Activity 5.3: Writing research questions correctly

1 There should be only one 'f' in 'professional'; only three 'e's in 'development'.
2 There is one misuse of the apostrophe, and confusion of affect/effect. The question should read: *In the opinion of teachers and students, what is the effect of music on behaviour?*

We look in more detail at common mistakes in the use of English in Chapter 12.

Activity 6.1: Vygotsky's ideas

There are many possible responses to this task. Here is one:

Brown (2003) pointed out that one of Vygotsky's main contributions to our understanding of learning is the concept of the 'zone of proximal development'. White (2006: 27) explained that this refers to the gap between what an individual can do alone and what can be achieved with 'knowledgeable others'.

There has been much discussion about the exact nature of these 'knowledgeable others'. Green (2008) felt that in most cases it means the teacher. Indeed, an observational study of 50 secondary-school classrooms by Lavender (2010) concluded that the teacher's role is crucially important in helping children to learn.

Others have taken a wider view. Black (2009) found in her study that a range of adults play an important role in children's learning. Gold (2010: 65) similarly concluded: 'When considering the important role of the teacher in Vygotsky's ideas, we must be careful not to devalue the contribution of others, such as assistants, parents, even peers'. Amber (2012: 34) has broadened this idea even further, highlighting the importance of communication if the child is to learn: 'It is dialogue which is important, the children must be able to exchange thoughts and ideas with others'.

To evaluate your own version, ask yourself or a friend:

- Is my version clear?
- Does one paragraph logically lead to the next?
- Have I drawn different literature together to show agreement or contrast in perspectives about particular ideas?

Activity 6.2: Trevor's literature review

*Early definitions of very able children, for example Rowlands (1974), stressed a child's current ability [1. **Useful historical perspective**]. However, Montgomery (1996) sought a definition which included what a child might achieve but did not yet demonstrate [2. **Interesting contrast**]. Similarly, Freeman (2001) said we should think of children in terms of their future rather than their present performance [3. **Useful agreement**]. This outlook has made it possible to stress the importance of providing challenging educational activities so that ability can emerge: students 'will rarely manifest high* *ability unless they have the opportunity to do so' (Fletcher-Campbell, 2003: 3)* [4. A well argued judgement, backed up by the literature]. *A recent official definition in England reflected this dual outlook: gifted and talented children are those 'with one or more abilities developed to a level significantly ahead of their year group (or with the potential to develop those abilities)' (Department for Children, Schools and Families, 2008: 6)* [5. Relevant definition which Trevor may be able to use as the basis for his project as a whole].

References

Department for Children, Schools and Families (2008) *Effective Provision for Gifted and Talented Children in Primary Education*. Revised ed. London: Department for Children, Schools and Families.

Fletcher-Campbell, F. (2003) 'The gifted and talented: who are they and does it matter who they are?' *Topic*, 30: 1–5.

Freeman, J. (2001) *Gifted Children Grown Up*. London: David Fulton.

Montgomery, D. (1996) *Educating the Able*. London: Cassell.

Rowlands, P. (1974) *Gifted Children and their Problems*. London: J.M. Dent & Sons.

Activity 8.1: Questions to avoid

A.	*Why is it important for children to play competitive sport?*	On its own this is a loaded question (7) – some respondents may feel it is not important for children to play sport of this kind.
B.	*What does the school development plan say about playground facilities?*	You could examine the plan yourself (2).
C.	*Do children have regular opportunities to read in your class?*	Yes/no question (1), and it is vague (5) or ambiguous (7) – what exactly does 'regular' mean?
D.	*Are you married and do you have children?*	This is a double question (6) – and do you really need this information (3)?
E.	*Do students think reading is OK?*	This is a yes/no question (1), it is vague (5) and you should be asking the students themselves (2).
F.	*What are the causes of boys' underachievement in schools?*	Are your respondents sufficiently knowledgeable to provide this information (4)? You could find this out better by examining research reports (2).
G.	*Why don't students pay attention if they sit at the back and can't see you and how do you deal with that when or if it happens?*	This is a double question (6), the first part would be better answered by students (2) and it is much too complicated (7).
H.	*What is the meening of education?*	This is too broad (5), and there is a spelling mistake (8).

Appendix II   Activity 8.1 Questions to avoid

Activity 10.1: Debbie's inappropriate letter

- Full address is needed.
- Full date is needed.
- Letter should be addressed to the principal (or headteacher or manager).
- Full address of college is needed.
- Letter should be addressed more formally: 'Dear Mr Jones'.
- Letter should be composed more formally.
- Debbie should introduce herself more fully, for example by giving her place of study, course and year.
- She should explain how her project is part of her course.
- She should give a better reason for wishing to do her project at this college, for instance because the college has a good reputation in the topic she is investigating.
- 'Talk' is mis-spelt.
- Use 'children' or 'students', not 'kids'.
- Debbie should offer to go to discuss her project at a time that is convenient for the college.
- She should use a more formal ending than 'love from'.
- Debbie should give her full name (and no kisses).
- She should say more clearly what her project is about, and put this in the main text of her letter.

Activity 11.1: Andrew's analysis of quantitative data

- So far, use of the Internet is overall the most popular – but one respondent places it last.
- Use of email is common, but not the most common for any individual.
- For two respondents, social networking is important, for others much less so.
- Writing notes does not score highly, but none of Andrew's respondents put it in last place.
- If Andrew had sufficient relevant data, he could, for instance, compare the responses of boys and girls, older and younger students, or those with different examination grades.

Activity 12.1: Find the referencing mistakes

In the text:

- The Finch citation needs the date.
- The Wren citation should not include the initial.
- Wren's quote needs the page number.

In the reference list:

- The Crow reference needs the place of publication and publisher.
- Finch reference: the title of the book needs italics (underlining is also possible, if used consistently).
- Swan reference: the date does not match the date in the text. The place of publication and the publisher are the wrong way round.
- The Swift and Jay reference is not cited in the text. The accessed date needs the year.
- The Chickadee reference needs the initial and is not in alphabetical order.
- The Wren reference needs the date.

Activity 12.2: Find the mistakes

This is how the text should look – the corrected words are in italics:

How does teaching *affect students'* learning? Is *practice* the most *effective* method? Students are different – one *student's* way of learning is not the way of other students. It depends *whose* opinion you listen *to. Children's* learning is very complicated, so the *principal* concern for a school is to pay attention to *its* work so that its *students* can learn *successfully.*

Appendix III
Glossary

Term	Definition	See Chapter
Abstract	A very short summary of a project: its topic, methods and main findings.	2, 12
Action research	Research which investigates everyday actions, in work or in our social lives, with a view to improving systems and practice. It is often carried out by practitioners themselves.	1
Active consent	This is where a participant actively agrees to take part, for instance by telling the researcher directly or signing a consent form.	9
Analysis	'The job of systematically breaking down something into its constituent parts and describing how they relate to each other' (Hart, 1998: 110). This process is an essential part of composing a literature review and of handling data.	6, 11
Anonymity	Concealing the identity of participants and anyone else mentioned in the data. This includes the name of the centre, school or college where the investigation is carried out.	8, 9
Bibliography	A list of material consulted while working on a project, or which is recommended for further reading. It is not the same as a reference list. Most projects do not require a bibliography.	12
Case study	An in-depth investigation of an individual, group, event or system, usually within its real-life context and sometimes over a period of time (called a 'longitudinal' study).	1
Cause and effect	Trying to find out if and how one thing causes or affects another (also termed 'causality').	1, 4
Central tendency	Typical or average values in a set of data. The mean, median and mode are measures of this.	11
Citation	The process of providing references in a text, to show where ideas and quotations have come from.	12
Closed questions	Questions which provide a range of answers from which respondents must choose.	8
Coding	'Coding is simply a process of classifying chunks of your interview data and observations into key themes or headlines' (Roberts-Holmes, 2011: 186–187).	11
Comparative research	Research which investigates two or more different situations, for instance practice in different countries or institutions, and makes comparisons in order to understand both situations better.	1
Confidentiality	The researcher's promise not to disclose original or 'raw' data from the research, only when those data have been analysed and anonymized.	8, 9
Continuous observation	Observing activity continuously, for instance everything one group of students does throughout a lesson.	8

Term	Definition	See Chapter
Criticality	The process of evaluating the quality, value and implications of ideas and how they are expressed. It helps to contribute in constructive ways to debate about them.	6
Data	The information obtained from research methods.	7, 11
Discourse analysis	Analysing conversations in very close detail: choice of vocabulary, tone of voice, how participants initiate or respond to dialogue.	11
Document analysis	Examining what people have written or created and using the results of analysis as data.	7
Ethical approval	This is given when those responsible assess and confirm a person's readiness to carry out research in ways which respect the rights and needs of the participants.	9
Ethics	Being 'ethical' means that the project does not cause harm or disadvantage to anyone who takes part, including the researcher. Ethical considerations apply to all aspects of a research project.	1, 4, 7, 12
Ethnography	Ethnographic research studies cultures or groups in naturalistic contexts. Ethnographic researchers often immerse themselves in the lives of those they are researching.	1
Evaluative research	Research which assesses the usefulness or effectiveness of an organization or activity, possibly to indicate whether it should continue.	1
Event-sampling	Watching continuously, but only recording something when it is seen happening. Such instances can be counted or described, or both.	8
Experimental research	Research involving a structured experiment. Situations are carefully organized, so that different scenarios can be investigated.	1
Exploratory research	Research which seeks to understand situations more clearly and deeply than before, often from varied perspectives.	1
Findings	What is discovered from data collected and analysed in response to the research questions.	2, 12
Focus group	A pre-determined group of people who debate amongst themselves issues raised by the researcher.	7
Generalizability	The extent to which findings apply, not just to the people who took part in the investigation and the setting where it was carried out, but to other people and other settings also.	11
Grounded theory	An approach to research, first formulated by Glaser and Strauss (1967), which is used to create or produce an overall theory from wide-ranging investigation.	1
Hypothesis	A statement which might be true (or might not). Researchers may set up a 'controlled trial' so that the strength of the statement can be examined.	5
Informed consent	Informed consent means two things: first, that those involved understand the nature of the research; second, that they agree to contribute to the research on this basis.	9
Interpretivism	A paradigm based on the belief that what we accept as real arises from the different perceptions of different people, interacting with complex social and physical environments. Truth is socially 'constructed' – we decide what it is – rather than existing independently of us.	1
Interval data	Categories of quantitative data ranked in precise order with measureable differences between them.	11
Interview framework	A list of questions to be asked and how they will be asked.	8

Term	Definition	See Chapter
Interviews	Conversations between researcher and interviewees, usually with the researcher asking questions which the interviewees answer or debate.	7
Literature	The books, articles and other published material which have already been written about the topic.	Introduction
Literature review	A literature review is a critical analysis of what is understood already about the topic and themes related to it, and of some of the varied perspectives which have been expressed.	2, 6, 12
Mean	The average of a set of quantitative data.	11
Median	The middle category point in a set of quantitative data.	11
Methodology	The range of methods and procedures used to investigate the topic and find answers to research questions.	2, 7, 12
Mode	The most common response in a set of quantitative data.	11
Nominal data	In quantitative data analysis, these are numbers assigned to unranked categories.	11
Non-participant observation	Observation where events are watched without getting personally involved.	7
n =	In analysis of quantitative data, the number of respondents whose data are presented.	11
Observation	Observation 'involves the researcher watching, recording and analysing events of interest' (Blaxter et al., 2010: 199).	7
Observation framework	A table or chart which helps to focus attention on what we wish to observe and on recording what we see.	8
Open questions	These questions allow respondents a free choice of how to respond and possibly to write at length about thoughts, opinions and experiences.	8
Ordinal data	Categories of quantitative data ranked in order but which (in research terms) are rather imprecise.	11
Originality	How the project contributes new knowledge and understanding.	4
Paradigms	The conscious and unconscious beliefs which underlie the questions we ask and the ways in which we carry out research, and which shape the kind of conclusions which emerge from our investigation.	1
'Paradigm wars'	Vigorous debate about which paradigm is most suitable for research.	1
Participant observation	Taking part in the event, such as a meeting, being observed.	7
Participants	Participants are those who take part in the research methods and provide data.	7
Periodic observation	Observing intensively for a few minutes, then taking a break; or at regular intervals noting down what those being observed are doing and ignoring what they are doing between those times. This is sometimes also called 'interval observation'.	8
Piloting	Testing out methods in advance and changing them as a result.	9
Plagiarism	Work presented as your own when in fact it is someone else's. Plagiarism is a serious wrongdoing in research and academic writing and, if discovered, consequences are severe.	12
Population	All those to whom research applies and who therefore could theoretically (with time and resources) be participants in an investigation.	7
Positivism	A research paradigm based on the idea that the world we are investigating has one stable and logical reality, and the purpose of investigation is to determine and measure this.	1

Term	Definition	See Chapter
Presumed consent	Telling participants about the research and asking them to say if they do not wish to participate. If they say nothing, it can be 'presumed' that they agree to participate. This may also be called 'passive consent'.	9
Primary data	Original data which are collected as part of an investigation.	7
Project tutor	Usually a university or college lecturer who has experience in doing research and who supports the researcher in their work (sometimes known as a 'supervising tutor' or 'supervisor').	2
Proofreading	Reading text to check that it is clear and fully accurate. It can be done by the researcher or by someone else.	2, 12
Qualitative data	Data consisting of words or visual images.	7, 11
Quantitative data	Data made up of numbers or quantities.	7, 11
Questionnaire	A set of written questions which participants answer in writing. This might involve choosing from a selection of responses, or writing sentences about information or opinions, or a mixture of both.	7
Range	The distance between two extremes of quantitative data.	11
Reference list	A list of all the material cited in a text. It is provided at the end of a project.	12
Referencing	Referencing involves acknowledging clearly where the ideas described, used and discussed have originated.	12
Reflective practice	Educators thinking hard about what they do, appraising its value and how it might be done better.	1
Relatability	This means that other people and settings, especially those similar to the participants and research venue, may well be able to learn and benefit from what has been found out.	11
Reliability	Reliability means that a method is free from error. When it is used repeatedly, it produces consistent results.	9, 12
Research	Purposeful investigation, aimed at finding out things we did not know before.	1
Research brief	A clear and concise summary of research which can be given to anyone who needs or wants to know about it.	9
Research design	A plan of what an investigation is about and how the researcher will investigate it.	2
Research instruments	These are the tools and resources used to collect and record your data. Examples are a questionnaire, a set of interview questions or a framework for observation.	8
Research log	A record of thoughts, concerns and ideas whilst undertaking a project.	2
Research proposal	A written outline, showing the nature of a research project and how the researcher plans to conduct it.	2
Research questions	The questions which are being answered in the investigation.	5, 12
Research topic	The theme, issue or problem which is being investigated in the research.	4
Research venue	The centre, school, college or other setting where the research is carried out.	2, 10
Respondents	Respondents are those who respond to questions in questionnaires or interviews and provide data.	7
Sampling	The process of deciding who will participate in an investigation. The participants chosen and who agree to take part are called the 'sample'.	7

Term	Definition	See Chapter
Secondary data	Data gathered as part of someone else's research, which we then use as part of our own investigation (referenced, of course).	7
Secondary referencing	Citing in the text a piece of literature which has been found cited elsewhere.	12
Semi-structured interviews	Interviews where the researcher plans some questions beforehand, but during the interview may ask additional questions, or discuss additional topics, not necessarily planned in advance.	7
Semi-structured observation	Observation where there is a particular area of interest and noting down events relating to this. However, other aspects may be recorded which seem interesting or relevant.	7
Standard deviation	'A measure of the extent to which values in a distribution cluster about the mean' (Muijs, 2011: 93).	11
Statistical significance	In analysis of quantitative data, a calculation which indicates whether a relationship between variables in the data is likely to have occurred by chance, or because that relationship really does exist or occur more widely.	11
Structured interview	An interview where the researcher prepares all questions in advance and the interviewee answers them one by one.	7
Structured observation	Observations where the researcher knows in advance exactly what he or she is looking out for.	7
Survey	A survey, for instance a questionnaire survey, involves collection of data about a particular topic from many respondents.	7
Systematic review	These reviews critically appraise a range of research evidence or literature (or both) on a particular topic.	1
Testing	Using a set of questions or problems to assess the abilities or performance of an individual or group.	7
Theoretical research	A type of research which scrutinizes concepts and ideas (such as equality and justice), rather than their practical application.	1
Triangulation	Triangulation means drawing data from two or more methods or sources, so that we can make use of varied perspectives to answer our research questions.	9
Unstructured interview	An interview where researcher and interviewee explore broad areas related to the research topic, without prior planning of questions.	7
Unstructured observation	Observing and recording everything that is happening for later analysis.	7
Validity	This is the extent to which an instrument measures what it is supposed to measure. Put another way, it is the extent to which an instrument helps a researcher to find out what she or he wishes to find out.	9, 12
Variables	Characteristics of data, such as the gender, age or ethnicity of sampled participants, or their experiences, achievements or opinions, which we are interested in investigating further.	1, 11
Viva	Presenting a project face-to-face to examiners and answering questions. The researcher explains, debates and 'defends' what he or she has done and written.	Conclusion
Vulnerable groups	Participants who may be particularly susceptible to inequality in relationships. They include children and young people, in particular those with disabilities, those who are physically or mentally ill, and those in care.	9

Index

Added to a page number:

'a' denotes Activity

'aa' denotes Activity Answers (Appendix II)

'c' denotes Case Study

'f' denotes Further Reading

'g' denotes Glossary (Appendix III)

'p' denotes Project Sheet (Appendix I)